Baghdad to Fallujah

# Baghdad to Fallujah

*Memoir of a U.S. Marine
in the Iraq War*

BRIAN VAN GORDEN

McFarland & Company, Inc., Publishers
*Jefferson, North Carolina*

All photographs are from the author's collection.

The views expressed in this publication are those of the author and do not necessarily reflect the official policy or position of the Department of Defense or the U.S. government. The public release clearance of this publication by the Department of Defense does not imply Department of Defense endorsement or factual accuracy of the material.

The names used in this book are pseudonyms for those below the rank of O6.

Library of Congress Cataloging-in-Publication Data

Names: Van Gorden, Brian, 1983– author.
Title: Baghdad to Fallujah : memoir of a U.S. Marine in the Iraq War / Brian Van Gorden.
Other titles: Memoir of a U.S. Marine in the Iraq War
Description: Jefferson, North Carolina : McFarland & Company, Inc., Publishers, 2024 | Includes index.
Identifiers: LCCN 2024025997 | ISBN 9781476693651 (paperback : acid free paper) ∞
  ISBN 9781476653471 (ebook)
Subjects: LCSH: Van Gorden, Brian, 1983- | Iraq War, 2003-2011—Personal narratives, American. | Iraq War, 2003-2011—Campaigns—Iraq. | United States. Marine Corps. Marine Regiment, 4th. Battalion, 3rd. Company K. | United States. Marine Corps. Marine Regiment, 4th. Battalion, 3rd. Scout Sniper Platoon. | Fallujah, Battle of, Fallūjah, Iraq, 2004. | Snipers—Iraq—Biography. | United States. Marine Corps—Biography.
Classification: LCC DS79.766 .V364 2024 | DDC 956.7044/342092 [B]—dc23/eng/20240614
LC record available at https://lccn.loc.gov/2024025997

British Library cataloguing data are available

**ISBN (print) 978-1-4766-9365-1**
**ISBN (ebook) 978-1-4766-5347-1**

© 2024 Brian Van Gorden. All rights reserved

*No part of this book may be reproduced or transmitted in any form or by any means, electronic or mechanical, including photocopying or recording, or by any information storage and retrieval system, without permission in writing from the publisher.*

Front cover image: Brian Van Gorden during the battle at the Diyala bridge, April 2003.

Printed in the United States of America

*McFarland & Company, Inc., Publishers*
 *Box 611, Jefferson, North Carolina 28640*
  *www.mcfarlandpub.com*

*To the men and women who fought
and died in the Iraq war*

"One of the things that I learned in the war is that we're not the top species on the planet because we're nice. We are a very aggressive species; it is in us. People talk a lot about how well the military turns kids into killing machines, and I'll always argue that it's just finishing school. What we do with civilization is that we learn to inhibit and rope in these aggressive tendencies, and we have to recognize them. I worry about a whole country that doesn't recognize them, because think of how many times we get ourselves into scrapes as a nation because we're always the 'good guys.' Sometimes, I think if we thought we weren't always the good guys, we might actually get into less wars."

—Karl Marlantes, *Vietnam War veteran and novelist*

# Table of Contents

*Introduction*     1

1. Boot Camp     3
2. School of Infantry     13
3. Training for War     22

**Deployment I:
Operation Iraqi Freedom
(January to June 2003)**

4. The Invasion     35
5. Diyala     47
6. Baghdad     57
7. Scout/Sniper Platoon     66

**Deployment II:
Operation Iraqi Freedom II
(January to July 2004)**

8. Haditha     79
9. The Battle for Fallujah     87
10. Halting the Advance     100
11. On the Hunt     112

## Table of Contents

## Deployment III:
## Operation Iraqi Freedom III
## (February to August 2005)

| | |
|---|---:|
| 12. Returning to Fallujah | 127 |
| 13. Blue on Blue | 140 |
| 14. Father's Day Massacre | 149 |
| 15. Home and Comfort | 162 |
| *Military History of the Author* | 171 |
| *Acronyms and Other Abbreviations* | 173 |
| *Index* | 175 |

# Introduction

The initial Karl Marlantes quote in this book on page vi is not to imply that the United States did not act in good faith during the Iraq War. I believed in what we were doing with hopes of creating a better life for the Iraqi people and a safer world overall. I know it sounds cliché; however, that is truly how I felt. I refuse to feel differently about it, especially knowing that thousands of lives were on the line. The quote was used to depict the complexity of conflicts in which a population can transition from ally to foe quickly and how the dominating force (i.e., American military) reacts to the ever-changing situation.

I was fresh out of high school when I found out about the September 11 attacks. It was early morning in 2001 and I remember seeing the twin towers on fire in New York city. Smoke was smoldering from where the terrorist-hijacked jumbo jet airplanes had collided into the buildings. The mood on the news felt very serious and I got the sense that it was not a typical terrorist attack. People were jumping from the tops of the towers as news poured in revealing the scope of the attack on the United States.

The Pentagon was attacked as well as the twin towers. I figured if the Pentagon had been attacked, that in itself was an act of war on behalf of the country directing the assaults on American soil. Having seen the seriousness of the situation unfolding, something deep down inside of me told me that we were headed for a war. I had a feeling that I would likely be a part of that war because I already had plans of joining the Marine Corps and I was not about to change my mind. I would speak to a Marine recruiter later that year and sign the final papers for my enlistment in December of 2001.

## Introduction

At that time in my life, it was hard to imagine just how involved I would be in the upcoming conflict. I truly did not know what to expect or even if that war would come. U.S. special forces would operate in Afghanistan shortly after the September 11 terrorist attacks as the intelligence gathered on behalf of the United States would indicate links that country. I thought that the war in Afghanistan might be limited strictly to air strikes and special forces skirmishes. The United States had not been engaged in a large-scale war that lasted more than a month since Vietnam and if that large war came, I thought that it might not be too different from Operation Desert Storm.

# 1

# Boot Camp

It was February 2002, and I was a recruit stationed at Camp Pendleton, California, also known as the Marine Corps Recruit Depot (MCRD). The day finally came for my boot camp platoon to be acquainted with our drill instructors or "DI's" as they were called. The instructors consisted of the head DI who was the rank of a staff sergeant and two other instructors who were the rank of sergeant. The head DI was a slightly chubby Hispanic guy who had served as a scout/sniper for the Marine Corps prior to becoming a drill instructor. The DI second in charge of our platoon was a skinny male Asian American who had served in the Fourth Marines as infantry. The remaining instructor was a tall, built, Caucasian guy who had served in Marine Corps Reconnaissance.

It was early morning as the platoon sat on the cold concrete floor inside of our barracks. The head DI introduced himself along with his fellow instructors. All the DI's appeared sharp and disciplined, which was an intimidating sight. I think most recruits are nervous when they arrive at Marine Corps boot camp for the first time due to not knowing what to truly expect. The head DI then went on to explain what he expected of us and how we were to conduct ourselves in boot camp. Every response from the recruits to the DI's had to be sharp, loud, and fast.

The initial week of boot camp can be summed up as gathering the necessary gear for training, punctuated by bouts of what one may think of as physical hazing to instill discipline within our platoon. It seemed as if every movement we conducted during boot camp was seen and corrected by the DI's. For example, one morning as the

# 1. Boot Camp

platoon stood in line for the chow hall, one of the recruits near me had slightly moved one of his arms toward his waist when he should have been standing at the position of attention. The position of attention consists of head forward, hands to your side, and looking straight ahead without unnecessary movement.

The arm movement by the recruit was immediately seen by a nearby DI who had been standing maybe twenty feet away. The angry DI then quickly approached him, grabbed the recruit's arm, and said, "You don't move that fucking arm unless I say so! You are supposed to be standing at the position of attention!" I stood there at attention and looking straight forward in hopes of not receiving the DI's unwanted criticism.

As the initial weeks of boot camp went on, recruits were taught to ensure that other members of the platoon were doing what they were supposed to. If a recruit was tired and falling asleep during a course of Marine Corps instruction, it was encouraged by the DI's for other members of the platoon to slap that recruit in the back of the head in order to keep him awake. If other recruits made a slight mistake such as not locking their foot lockers or properly making their racks in the morning, the DI's would punish all members of the platoon in order to encourage group alignment to their expectations.

Within the first month of bootcamp, I had been picked as first squad leader for the platoon; therefore, I was typically visible to all DI's as we marched from area to area around MCRD. It was midafternoon in about the third week of boot camp as the platoon was hurriedly shuffled around the recruit depot for the reoccurring classroom instruction. As we waited around for the upcoming course of Marine Corps knowledge, I had the sudden urge to pee. I drank a lot of water earlier that day and there was no bathroom in sight. It was not like I could break formation and leave to use the restroom to relieve myself. The sensation to pee got so bad that I began grabbing my crotch area to distract from the stinging sensation of a full bladder. It had been very difficult to stay still as I tried to contain this urge, and my groin grabbing while in formation had been spotted by a nearby DI from another platoon.

The DI from the other platoon then rapidly walked up to me and

## 1. Boot Camp

said, "What the fuck do you think you're doing?!" The DI who was second in charge of our platoon quickly approached me due to the commotion. He then asked the DI from the other platoon what happened, and he angrily explained the situation. "You got your recruit here grabbing his dick and shit!" as he mimicked my movements to his crotch area.

I then told the drill instructors that I had to pee very bad and neither cared. My platoon DI then grabbed me and put me in the rear of first squad, causing me to lose my spot as first squad leader. I was then approached by the DI who was third in charge of the platoon in which he mentioned something along the lines of having the discipline to hold my pee and sitting inside a fox hole. I really did not care to hear what any of the DI's had to say at that moment because my only concern was to keep from urinating in my trousers. I would eventually utilize a nearby bathroom when the platoon was given a break from classroom instruction which averted the potential disaster of pissing my pants in boot camp.

While still in the initial stages of recruit training, I would find myself sitting in the reception area for dental. It was early morning and about the fourth week of boot camp as I sat in the comfort of a chair in the Navy medical building. My body felt tired as I sat there waiting to be seen by the dentist and fighting the urge to sleep. Before I knew it, my chin had settled on my chest and I was sound asleep.

In what seemed like no time at all, I was being slapped in the face with my Marine Corps cover, much in the way someone would smack a person back and forth on the face with a glove. "Wake up motherfucker!" I heard this random drill instructor shout while standing over me. "Aye, sir!" I shouted as I quickly sat up in my chair and appeared as alert as I possibly could. The drill instructor then walked away to complete his errand. Being corrected by other DI's was a common occurrence at MCRD as discipline was not only carried out by your regular instructor.

When the time came to get our rifles from the depot armory, the platoon formed a line early one morning as we awaited our new equipment. The recruits would then be hurried along as rifles were issued with gun cleaning kits. When I was eventually assigned an M-16, I was

## 1. Boot Camp

amazed at how large it seemed. I had never fired an assault rifle up to that point in my life and it felt like I was holding something powerful. My experience with firearms prior to that day included the use of small caliber shotguns and .22 caliber rifles with my father when we would go camping. The M-16 rifles issued to the platoon were the A-2 models which appeared old and worn. It was obvious that the rifles had been used many times before by other platoons that came before us.

A little after a month into boot camp, I noticed that my ankles were swelling up and were red with tenderness. With the swelling came bruising which in turn became painful as I would try to walk around as the platoon completed its day-to-day tasks. The pain in my ankles became so much that I eventually brought it up to the head DI one morning. He took one look at my ankles and ordered me to go to medical later that day.

After arriving at medical, it was discovered that I had cellulitis around my ankles and was ordered by the Navy Corpsman to stay in bed for approximately one week. There was to be no physical fitness or any other kind of training during this rest period. On about the second day of my bed restriction, I was approached by the Reconnaissance DI from my platoon who pointed out my condition to my peers while they were inside the barracks. "Look at him, in bed like a little bitch. Good recruit Van Gorden, I'll get the training out of you." I then thought, "Are you kidding me?! My ankles nearly disappeared, and I was ordered to be in bed!" However, I knew it was the DI's job to "motivate" me into recovery with a little bit of peer pressure tossed in for good measure.

I would eventually recover from my bout of cellulitis fairly quickly with the help of antibiotics. Once fully recovered, I was immediately thrusted back into training with my platoon. With the recent acquisition of our M-16 rifles, the platoon was regularly ordered to formation inside of our barracks. All the bed racks and foot lockers would be moved aside to make room for our drill practice.

Once formed up, our DI running the drill would put on music from his personal stereo while he stood in front of our formation. He would usually play Disturbed's "Down with the Sickness" as he would

# 1. Boot Camp

shout and perform drill movements with his rifle. The platoon would then follow the drill instructor's lead as the music played on for motivation. It was exciting for me as an 18-year-old to conduct rifle drill while listening to heavy metal music in the background.

One of the many aspects of boot camp training included the Marine Corps Martial Arts Training Program or MCMAP as it was called for short. Members of the platoon would meet in formation in the designated martial arts area to conduct the training movements coordinated by the certified MCMAP instructor of the day. Members of the platoon would then pair up with each other while conducting warm up and performing the movements taught during that segment. The warmup period consisted of exercises in which the recruits would collide their forearms together to kill or numb the nerve endings in the impacted area.

On one particular day of MCMAP, a recruit from our platoon who had been known to cry during physical training was paired up with another recruit from a sister platoon. The recruit from the sister platoon was a guide (lead recruit for that platoon) and was known to have plenty of prior martial arts training. Guides were typically chosen for their mental/physical toughness and were often relied upon to keep their respective platoons in line with the DI's orders. Once the warmup for MCMAP started, both recruits conducted the forearm numbing strikes to each other's arms. The recruit from our platoon began crying after about the third strike.

Several DI's were standing around both recruits as they performed the numbing movements. The guide from the other platoon simply looked at him while the recruit from my platoon was crying as the nearby DI's called him "a little bitch" and yelled at the guide to not to go easy on him. I kind of felt bad for him; however, he did seem to weep at the slightest sign of opposition during any kind of physical training. I believe the DI's from my platoon paired the two up in order to toughen up their recruit.

Other duties often assigned to a recruit during Marine Corps boot camp was the task of "fire watch." A recruit would stand post in the barracks at night while other members of the platoon would sleep. The recruit would then stay at the fixed post near the main entrance

# 1. Boot Camp

of our squad bay and would challenge any person entering. More often than not, it would be a DI entering and questioning a recruit about his general orders. This was then followed by some form of hazing. On one evening, I was assigned fire watch duty at which time a Marine Corps captain walked into the barracks.

Naturally, I challenged him as previously taught, and he immediately asked me about my general orders. He then asked if I had a problem with him as he proceeded to tell me that I had looked at him like I wanted to fight. "Let's step outside and take care of this," he sternly stated. What he said slightly confused me because I did not think I was looking at him in any particular way. I had been looking straight forward at the position of attention. I refused to step outside with him, as I was sure this was some sort of trap that would have been used an excuse for my DI's to haze me, had they heard I fought with a higher-ranking officer.

As boot camp continued, the platoon would continuously practice drill on the parade deck at MCRD, day in and day out. One evening, while the platoon was rehearsing drill for an upcoming battalion inspection, one of the recruits conducted a movement out of unison. The platoon had been doing very well up to that point and the unfortunate misstep conducted by the recruit was seen by the DI leading the drill. He immediately called a halt to the platoon's march and shouted at us to go to attention. The DI then walked right up to the recruit and without hesitation, quickly punched him in the stomach. I heard the recruit let out a gasp as he fought to breathe in air. The DI told the recruit to correct himself and the platoon continued with the drill for the evening.

The day would eventually come when the platoon would participate in the battalion inspection on the parade deck. The drill performance was judged by other DI's and members of the higher command at the recruit depot. Platoons in the battalion would be judged on factors to include marching, rifle drill, and uniform appearance. When the inspection was completed, I felt that our platoon did fairly well that day as we marched our way back to the barracks. Once in the squad bay, we were told to sit down in formation as our DI left the building to find out the results of our platoon's performance.

## 1. Boot Camp

About five minutes later, our DI returned and stood over us without any expression. His face was stoic as he calmly stated, "Our platoon placed second." He then immediately shoved a stack of foot lockers that he was standing behind as hard as he could onto the squad bay floor. "Well, it's not fucking good enough!" he shouted as he quickly walked out of the barracks. The platoon just sat there quietly. I figured we had some "physical training" coming our way soon for not having placed first in the inspection.

The platoon did eventually pay in terms of physical training for having placed second in the battalion inspection; however, this was a usual occurrence in boot camp. On one afternoon, the recruits from my platoon were being punished quite severely for the imperfections committed that morning. I had been coping with a nasty cough and a sore throat from the relentless "physical training." We had been ordered to continuously take apart and rebuild the metal frames of our bunk beds as we cleaned the barracks floor. When the racks were disassembled, we grabbed towels and placed them on the ground with both arms facing downward to hold them in place.

We then had to stand on our feet while holding the aforementioned towel; therefore, most of the pressure had been placed on our arms as we were then ordered to run across the squad bay with only our feet and arms making contact with the ground. This exercise was very tiring as the burning sensation in my arms and legs built up without almost any rest. The running with the towels seemed almost non-stop and this exacerbated my coughing which also made my sore throat that much more painful. We were continuously shouting "Aye, sir!" with each command given by the DI's until the task of cleaning the squad bay was finally completed to standard. I eventually made my way to the bathroom where I was able to cough and spit into the sink in an attempt to clear my throat. The phlegm that followed was mixed with blood as it flung out of my mouth.

The hazing from the DI's at MCRD would come and go. I would always look forward to receiving mail during bootcamp because it was nice to get letters from my family and friends. One afternoon, I would receive mail in which my mom had sent me some family photos. After receiving the mail, it was customary for the DI's to have the

# 1. Boot Camp

recruits line up along the wall near their den and look through any photos the recruits received. The recruits with any photographs were then ordered to line up along the wall as usual that afternoon as the instructors performed their review.

When my turn came up, the lead DI glanced at the photographs I had in my possession and then pointed to a lady while asking who that person was. I looked at the photo he held and told him that it was my mother. "That's your mom?!" repeated the DI. I told him yes and he replied, "You're fucking kidding me! That's your mom?!" I again told him yes as he showed the other instructors.

I did not think there was anything special about the photograph, which was a typical family picture. Later that evening when it was time to drink our canteens of water prior to bed, the recruits made their usual toasts to the Marine Corps as we would each take a swig. We as recruits would toast to Chesty Puller, the Marine Corps, and other Marine Corps heroes that had come before. For the last toast, one of the DI's stated, "Here's to Van Gorden's mom!" as the other recruits shouted in unison and drank their water.

Being made to consume water just before it was time to sleep was a nightly ritual at MCRD. It was yet another night in the barracks as the platoon did their usual toast to the Marine Corps. The recruits were drinking water from their canteens when the silence in the room was interrupted by the sound of a loud gag, followed by the noise of water splashing onto the barracks floor. One of the recruits had thrown up while drinking from his canteen. He continued throwing up as one of the DI's approached him and ordered him to drink his water. "You better fucking finish all of it!" the instructor demanded as the recruit attempted to gulp what water he had left.

In the final weeks of bootcamp, my platoon transitioned to Edson Range at Camp Pendleton, where we would shoot our rifles and learn basic patrolling tactics. There were also plenty of ruck marches in the nearby hills which had been arduous and tiring. On one afternoon, the platoon conducted what was probably an eight-mile hike with full gear. Once we had returned to the battalion staging area near the barracks, I heard one of the recruits grunting directly behind me. I turned

## 1. Boot Camp

around and saw him quickly pull out his penis from his trousers as he began peeing on the tarmac.

Apparently, he had to pee so bad that he was unable to hold it in. He just peed right there in front of the platoon and the instructors in broad daylight. A DI approached the recruit, looked him directly into his face, and stated, "Good motherfucker! You're done when we get back!" "Aye, sir!" replied the recruit. Once the platoon returned to the barracks, the recruit who had relieved himself was thoroughly "trained" in the form of physical exercises later that afternoon.

On one evening during field week, the platoon was positioned along a hillside near Edson Range. At this time, the platoon was setting up their half shelter tents in a rushed manner as one of the DI's did the typical restrictive countdown to number one in order to complete the task at hand. As our time dwindled, the DI shouted "Freeze!" Just before the order was given, I had apparently moved at the last second as I tried to come to the position of attention. The DI had seen my movement from about ten yards away and started walking angrily in my direction.

As soon as he approached me, he picked up a nearby five-gallon water jug and walked right up to my face while saying, "I thought I said fucking freeze!" as he then splashed water from the jug onto my utility uniform. It was probably thirty degrees out and I was now drenched. After receiving the soaking, I made my way to my half shelter tent as I tried to get some sleep. I was very uncomfortable, and I did not sleep very well that evening.

The platoon was about two weeks out from the Crucible as we completed mandatory courses of instruction at Edson Range. It seemed as though we were constantly doing physical training and getting punished for the slightest of mistakes with more frequency. One afternoon, the platoon was receiving chow from the mess hall, and it seemed as though all of the recruits within our platoon had grabbed full plates of food. As we prepared to sit down to eat, our DI found a reason to interrupt what we were doing and ordered every recruit in our platoon to throw away their food. I had only taken one bite out of my apple when I poured all the food on my plate into a large nearby trash can. I think the platoon had been punished because one of the

# 1. Boot Camp

recruits may not have held his cup of milk or water with both hands. Therefore, the platoon paid for that mistake and was not able to eat that afternoon.

The days spent at Edson Range seemed to drag on due to the continuous ruck marches and punishments dealt out by the DI's. When the final day of the Crucible eventually came, our battalion marched toward the final mountain we would hike for what would be the remainder of the course before earning the right to be called a United States Marine. Our packs would be completely full as we marched off in the early morning from our rest site. I was tired as I am sure the other recruits were as we pushed on with the remainder of the course. As we approached the mountain, my back began to cramp as the battalion kept the steady pace on the upward slope. I could hear the heavy breathing coming from the recruits as they strained to catch their breaths. The DI's could be heard yelling at the recruits to keep up as several recruits began to fall behind.

When we finally reached the top of the mountain, I felt a huge sense of relief. I knew that as soon as we completed the Crucible, we could finally eat a large meal and we would no longer need to perform long hikes for the remainder of boot camp. Several recruits had tears streaming down their faces as they appeared proud of what they just accomplished. I did not cry at the completion of the course; however, I did feel like I had achieved something worthwhile.

# 2

# School of Infantry

The recruit battalion I was in would eventually make its way back to MCRD in preparation for our Eagle, Globe, and Anchor ceremony, just prior to boot camp graduation. The ceremony would take place on the morning of May 2002 at the recruit depot parade deck. It was a rather emotional time for the former recruits as well as myself because we were about to officially become United States Marines. Some of the Marines in my platoon were shedding tears and others simply appeared proud to have finally gained the title.

Our DI would approach each member of the platoon in sharp military fashion by conducting drill movements to face each Marine personally while handing out the emblems. Once the DI marched in my direction and faced me, he immediately had a smirk on his face. He congratulated me on becoming a United States Marine and with the same smirk, he asked if my family was on the parade grounds to see me. I replied, "Yes, sir." He then asked, "Is your mom here?" I again replied, "Yes, sir" while trying not to laugh in formation. The DI simply kept his smile and turned to march toward the next Marine in the squad.

It was humorous to think that on such an important day, at least for the former recruits, the DI remembered to ask if my mother showed up for my graduation ceremony. I shrugged off the thought and continued to stand in formation while feeling relieved that boot camp was practically over. During the ceremony, my platoon was given the title of "Honor Platoon" because we had the best overall performance to include drill, rifle qualification, and physical training. The Eagle, Globe, and Anchor ceremony marked the beginning of a new period in my life, and it was a gratifying feeling of accomplishment. I was happy

## 2. School of Infantry

to know that my family was there to celebrate such an occasion with me. My family would continue to play a vital role in the upcoming events during my time in the Marine Corps.

After the Eagle, Globe, and Anchor ceremony, my platoon was released from formation to spend time with their families around the MCRD grounds. I was walking around the depot with my mom inside of the base's Marine Corps Exchange (MCX) and had bought a small snack with an apple. After buying the snack, I walked outside into a common area near the store and began eating my apple while talking with my mother. A nearby random DI then quickly approached me and pulled me aside. Under his breath he asked, "Why the fuck are you eating an apple in uniform?!"

It had not crossed my mind at the time I was eating it; however, he was right. Marines were not allowed to stand and eat while in dress uniform in public. I told him that it was a mistake while proceeding to throw my apple away in the trash can. Once the DI walked away, he approached my platoon instructor, the one who had been in the 4th Marines, who was also nearby, and apparently told him what just happened. I returned to my mom, and she asked what occurred. I told her that I had been eating when I shouldn't have been. I then continued to enjoy my free time with my family.

Even with the completion of the Eagle, Globe, and Anchor ceremony, there was still some time to be spent at boot camp prior to receiving my Military Occupational Specialty (MOS) training. The following morning after becoming a Marine, I was approached by my platoon DI while I was in the barracks. He then ordered me to the position of attention while asking why I had eaten food while standing in dress uniform the day prior. He then went on to say, "I had to hear it from that asshole from the other platoon! You know I don't like that motherfucker!" After receiving the correction from the DI, I was ordered to get back to what I was doing.

Upon the completion of Marine Corps boot camp, the Marines who recently graduated were given a leave period before either attending the Marine Corps School of Infantry (SOI) or Marine Combat Training (MCT). The Marines with an infantry MOS, or "grunts" as they were sometimes referred to, would be assigned to the School of

## 2. School of Infantry

Infantry for approximately two months before going to their battalion of assignment. Marines with an MOS other than infantry, or "POGs" (Person Other than Grunts), would be assigned to Marine Combat Training for approximately one month before they would receive their primary MOS training.

After my leave period upon completion of boot camp, I would return to Camp Pendleton to attend the School of Infantry training. It was a sunny morning in June of 2002, when my stepfather and I arrived at Pendleton in his car. My stepfather was there to drop me off at the check-in area of the school. I was somewhat nervous because I had just recently completed boot camp and was anticipating what was to come next. Would it be harder than boot camp, I wondered as we approached the barracks building. I could see other Marines who recently graduated boot camp walking around the SOI area in their Class "C" uniforms. Once I was dropped off, I was seated in a large room with other Marines who were also attending the school. The Marine checking us in was a stocky Corporal. He walked around the room while talking very loudly; however, not with the usual drill instructor intensity.

It was a calmer, but stern voice. He called out individual Marine names as he passed out sheets for us to fill out. He eventually called out my name while standing next to me. When I responded, he gave me one of the pieces of paper to write on. I was still pretty nervous, and my mouth was dry. This was made more apparent when the instructor very boisterously told me that my breath stank when I answered him.

Once I completed my check in, I was assigned to my respective company for training. I would be settled in with my wall locker and bunk bed that I would share with another Marine. The environment in the School of Infantry was a little bit more relaxed than bootcamp. The instructors didn't yell at you quite as much and not everything in your daily life was completely dominated by count down instruction. I guess you can say that we were treated with slightly more respect by the instructors and other senior Marines, but not by a whole lot. We were still considered new guys or "boots" and had not even really begun to experience what the Marine Corps was about.

## 2. School of Infantry

I would share my bunk with a tall male Caucasian Marine by the name of Brad. He was about the same age as me and had come from Oklahoma. He had a slight twang in his voice; however, I still understood him when he spoke. We would become good friends from the beginning of the training throughout my four-year Marine Corps enlistment. When weekend leave came during training, I would invite him over to my house so that he would not have to hang out at the barracks; plus we enjoyed each other's company.

The gear that Marines were issued in SOI such as our Kevlar helmets, flak vests, and most of the weapons we trained with were run down by prior use. The gear and weapons appeared to work fine; it was just obvious that they were continuously handed down from each training battalion. The barracks buildings there were large multi-story structures containing the wall lockers for each Marine with two-man bunks lined neatly in rows. The living quarters were much nicer than the conditions I experienced in boot camp, and it was a welcomed progressive change.

The training during SOI would come quickly. It was around late June 2002 when the class was to perform their land navigation course. The course consisted of finding your way to several designated points by the use of a compass, map, and protractor with a string. Upon reaching each point, there was a way to confirm each location, which you wrote down to show the instructor later that day for verification. The land navigation checkpoints would be spread out over several miles on the Camp Pendleton base and would include several terrain features. We were instructed to immediately report back to the instructors and to shout out a specific phrase in order to show we completed the course.

The land navigation course would start early in the morning. I felt somewhat confident that I understood how to navigate to the checkpoints utilizing the compass and map. I also liked hiking so that was a plus. I grabbed my gear and headed out for the points from the main classroom on base. As I set out, I reached my first checkpoint with relative ease while continuing my trek through the Camp Pendleton shrubbery. I would eventually complete the course and return to the classroom with my verification codes from each location. I waited in

## 2. School of Infantry

line with the other Marines who completed the training as I awaited my turn to approach the instructor. I handed him my verification codes and he replied, "What the fuck were you supposed to say?!"

I forgot to say the phrase given to the class by the instructors. "Good! You're going to do it again!" Since I had not approached the instructor with the designated phrase they had asked for earlier, I was immediately told to do the course again the following day. I was upset because I was sure I had reached each of my checkpoints, but at that time it did not matter. I would complete the land navigation course the following day and reach each location without issue. However, I made sure to shout out the necessary phrase when the time came to check in with the instructor.

One morning, the SOI company leadership decided that instead of running for physical training that day, the Marines should participate in a large-scale wrestling match while in our shirts and BDU pants. The match would take place inside a large circle containing wood chips typically used by the Marine Corps Martial Arts instructors. The idea was that Marines in our company would try to throw other Marines out of the large circle and whoever was the last one inside would be the winner. As we were given permission to fight, Marines frantically tried to throw each other out of the aforementioned circle.

The bout would go on for at least ten minutes until two Marines remained. To decide the winner, the two Marines would participate in a slapping match. Whenever one slapped the other so hard that he fell down, the Marine left standing would then be declared the winner. Both guys who remained were stocky and looked like they could slap very hard. When their match started, each Marine attempted to get the upper hand by positioning for a strike. One of them began to swing wildly with both hands until he connected directly with the side of the other Marine's face. The slap was very loud, and you could see the eyes of the Marine who had been struck go blank as he then fell back onto the wood chips. The Marine who won then threw both of his arms in the air with excitement while yelling in celebration.

As some time went by during SOI, I was able to purchase my first car, a green Pontiac Sunfire, from my older sister. The car was inexpensive, and I was excited to have it. This Pontiac would be my

## 2. School of Infantry

freedom from base. My family did not live far from Camp Pendleton; therefore, I would usually visit them when I had the chance.

Throughout the course of infantry training, the instructors would introduce us to the use of the M203 grenade launcher. The M203 was an under attachment to the M-16 rifle which was used typically in an anti-personnel role. We were also taught to use the M249 Squad Automatic Weapon (SAW) light machine gun. The use of shoulder fired rocket launchers, or AT-4s as they are known, was another part of our training, along with the application of live grenades.

In SOI, there was an emphasis on fire and maneuver tactics. There was one drill in particular I recall that was rather tiring. With full gear, a squad of Marines would bound and assault a fortified position. The maneuver was about one hundred yards in length and when the objective was successfully assaulted, the squad would quickly run back to the starting position of the course. It would get very hot when conducting the exercise and it was not a favorite of the Marines who were performing the training. This type of exercise would be emphasized throughout my time in the Marine Corps.

Since attending infantry training, I purposefully attempted to regain some of the weight I lost during boot camp. I was not comfortable with the idea of being skinny when there were other Marines who were rather large. This gain in weight would not be without any repercussions though. I probably went from about 155 pounds to roughly 180 pounds in a rather short period of time. We would conduct plenty of ruck marches in the hills surrounding Camp Pendleton that would go on for miles. By the end of most of the hikes, my inner thighs were chafed raw, which made it difficult to walk in a normal manner while in the healing process.

Inspections at this time were typical. One afternoon while in the barracks, one of the instructors searched the wall locker of another Marine. This Marine was a blond-haired kid, short in stature, and very skinny. Some might call him a "nerd" or a "geek." I think he may have come from the Midwest. As we stood at the position of attention for this inspection, very similar to what was experienced in boot camp, the instructor could be heard yelling, "What the fuck is this? Are you fucking kidding me?! Is that a pocket pussy?!" Several Marines could

## 2. School of Infantry

be heard trying unsuccessfully to contain their laughter. The instructor then went on to tell the Marine that it was contraband and that he would not be allowed to be in possession of the jelly-like vaginal replica sex toy.

With the inspections came the usual look at the photographs pinned up on the doors of our wall lockers. A Marine who lived in the Quartz Hill area close to Palmdale was in possession of a picture showing three girls dressed in bikinis. They were about nineteen years old and had great bodies. The instructor then told the Marine, "How the fuck did your fat ass get a picture of them?!" He then eventually made his way to my locker where I had a photo of my then wife Stephanie. She was wearing lingerie and posing. The instructor looked at it while giving a nod of approval.

I had married young after boot camp, like many other of the Marines who attended SOI. Prior to joining the Marine Corps, I attended church almost every Sunday and thought that marrying the first girl I had slept with was the right thing to do. I figured I would eventually have children with this woman, and we were both in the military. Stephanie was in the Army National Guard, so the thought of her having to deploy to any foreign country was not really taken into consideration at that time.

During Infantry training at Camp Pendleton, the fresh Marines were often regarded as "9/11 babies" and we were told by the instructors that they had a slight respect for us because we had joined almost immediately after the September 11, 2001, terrorist attacks. By doing so, we were told that we knew we had enlisted in the United States Marine Corps with the knowledge that we would likely be fighting a war in the Middle East. This is true for the most part, but regardless of 9/11, I always wanted to join the United States military. I felt that the military was in my soul as I have had many relatives who had fought in the United States military from the Civil War, World War I, World War II and Korea.

However, when the World Trade Centers and Pentagon were attacked on September 11, I had a feeling from that moment that I would likely be involved in a war and that my life would never be the same. It was a very strange feeling that I can't fully describe. I was just

## 2. School of Infantry

a 17-year-old high school kid who had no idea that he would be thrust into the frontlines of combat. The likes of which have not been seen or experienced by the United States military since the conflict that raged in Southeast Asia.

The last training exercise during SOI was conducted at a fictitious urban area located at Camp Pendleton. There we learned the basics of clearing buildings, crossing streets, and communicating in this type of landscape. The idea of having to fight in urban terrain was daunting to say the least. Rooms must be cleared systematically, and you can be shot from almost every angle. It was a very three-dimensional type of fighting. Everything from rooftops to sewer systems could be used by both sides to try and gain the upper hand. Battles such as Hue in Vietnam or Stalingrad in World War II were brought up by training cadre as examples of how tough and nasty urban fighting can be. Most of the emphasis of training for Military Operations on Urban Terrain (MOUT) was placed on Hue as it was the United States Marines who fought that battle in 1968.

In the final week of infantry training, one of the instructors challenged another Marine, who would soon be assigned to the Reconnaissance Battalion, to a slap fight inside of the barracks. It was all for fun and the Marines in the barracks quickly formed a circle around both men. As the match began, both began to shuffle around each other as each one exchanged a slap here and there to each other's faces. The instructor was a short stocky blonde guy in his mid-twenties and the Marine in our company was tall, young, and lanky, but in good shape. He had the reach on the instructor; however, neither could slap the other so hard that one would fall to the ground. The match would eventually end without a clear winner. These skirmishes between Marines were commonplace as they were an outlet for the some of the frustration of being away from home and the testosterone that would build up from being in such a male dominated environment.

A large portion of the Marines in my training company would be assigned to the 3rd Battalion 4th Marines in Twenty-Nine Palms, California, as their infantry unit of assignment. Others would be assigned to the Light Armored Reconnaissance unit at Camp Pendleton and fewer would be sent to Hawaii. Some of the Marines were upset that

## 2. School of Infantry

they were assigned to the Twenty-Nine Palms base, known as the Marine Corps Air Ground Combat Center (MCAGCC), because the area was known as less than desirable throughout the Marine Corps. The base there was located in the middle of a hot desert with little infrastructure in the surrounding areas. I was also assigned to the Twenty-Nine Palms base; however, I did not mind. My parents' house was only three hours away and I was used to living in the desert.

# 3

# Training for War

It was a hot summer's day in August of 2002 as I walked off the Greyhound bus and onto the hot tarmac of the 3rd Battalion 4th Marines headquarters. I had just arrived at my unit upon successful completion of my two-month infantry training. I was an 18-year-old infantryman and was still unsure of exactly what I had gotten myself into. The weather was extremely hot, well into the 100s, and my new station was in the middle of the Mojave Desert. I did not feel too secluded as my hometown was a short drive away; however, I could have only imagined what it must have been like for the Marines who had lived out of state.

Amenities such as entertainment were minimal and the closest city that was seen as tolerable for weekend excursions by most Marines was Palm Springs. The weather was almost always miserable in terms of heat and dry as a bone. With the bad reputation that the Marine Corps Air Ground Combat base had as it pertained to "fun" (deserved and undeserved), it was still the premier training grounds for the Corps in regards to desert warfare. The 9/11 attack was still fresh in the collective conscious of the United States and it seemed appropriate to have been assigned to a desert fighting infantry unit.

Upon checking in with headquarters, I along with several other newly arrived Marines was quickly taken by the duty NCO (Non-Commissioned Officer) to the barracks building that somewhat resembled a college dormitory. The housing was all concrete and steel, with rooms facing either north or south. Typically, each room had a total of three Marines consisting of the lance corporals on down to the privates. I was assigned to my room with two other grunts, one

## 3. Training for War

of whom was a thin, shy Hispanic kid who spoke broken English and the other an outspoken, tall, lanky kid of Russian descent. I say "kid" because like me, the Marines I just mentioned were only 18, maybe 19 years old.

As I settled into my room and had all my gear organized into my wall locker, I stepped outside of the small, boxed room that I called my living quarters and out onto the barracks balcony. I leaned over onto the concrete ledge and was suddenly overwhelmed by a feeling of loneliness. The sun was setting, the weather was warm, and all I could see beyond the base was desert. I stood there thinking, "What's next?" I thought that four years of this lifestyle was a long time as I had no prior life experience to compare it to. I then looked to my right and toward the MCX, which was located on the western portion of the base. I remember thinking, "Is this all I have for entertainment?" It seemed as though the stigma associated with the Twenty-Nine Palms Marine Corps base was already beginning to manifest itself and it was only day one for me.

The following Monday I would meet with my respective company. I was assigned to Kilo Company, 1st squad. The 3rd Battalion 4th Marines consisted of five companies, Headquarters & Service, India, Kilo, Lima, and Weapons. My initial job within Kilo Company 1st squad was as a basic rifleman, until I was told differently later that evening when Marines had gathered for a company muster. The platoon commander for Kilo Company was a tall and educated man in his early twenties. His name Lt Edmund and he was a graduate of the United States Naval Academy but had a baby face. After the muster, Lt Edmund pulled me aside and advised me that I was his new radio operator. He did not give me much explanation as to why, other than, "We are going into combat soon and I need someone who is smart enough to work that radio." All I can think of was, "Shit! I did not join the Marine Corps to talk on a radio!" However, I knew I had no choice and that the decision had already made.

My time spent at the Marine Corps Air Ground Combat Center would consist of plenty of rucksack marches, radio operator training, and field exercises. The morning formation runs started at about five o'clock on weekdays. The runs were anywhere from three to five

## 3. Training for War

miles at a moderate pace, followed by the incorporation of push-ups, pull-ups, and sit-ups. There was very little weight training added to the morning regiment, if any. That was to be done on our own time. The focus was cardiovascular, which would come into play later on.

The infantry training I received shortly after arriving at the Twenty-Nine Palms base focused a lot on fire and maneuver, which I had been introduced to in SOI. We would do company sized training days in the desert. There was a vast stretch of land that would reach out tens of miles and would meet with the bottom of a rocky mountain range near the barracks on base.

Other training drills were run by squads consisting of about nine men, all wearing full combat gear, including camouflage uniform, Kevlar helmet, flak vest, typically four, 30-round magazines to capacity for the M16-A2 (approximately two drums of ammo for the light machine gunners), a rifle, and other items chosen to have on your person. Some of the drills would start off with one person at a time so that each man could hone his skills in that particular training exercise. The squad would gather at the designated standby area to await their turn. As soon as the Marine was given the word, he would run out into the desert as if assaulting an enemy position.

He would sprint for a short period of time with the intent of closing in on an imagined enemy objective and seeking cover, also known as micro-terrain in the desert. Micro-terrain is the small mounds of dirt or small boulders that could be used as cover from incoming small arms fire. The Marine would then sprint with the mantra in mind that would allow him to know when it's time to stop rushing forward and to seek cover. "I'm up, he sees me, I'm down!" would be chanted in our heads as we assaulted our imagined foe.

On one specific hot summer night, Kilo Company was conducting this fire and maneuver exercise, with the emphasis on night training. Just before the exercise started, I took some caffeine pills so that I would be energized for the low-light exercise. The pills kicked in rather quickly and I was up for my run. Just as I was told to go, I sprinted into the warm desert with all my gear and ready to take the objective. "I'm up, he sees me, I'm down!" and I would hit the ground near the closest mound of desert dirt I could find. I would then shoot

## 3. Training for War

at the plastic target that appeared and then prop myself up for the next sprint.

Repeating the guiding mantra in my head would provide me with the signal to get back to the ground and shoot. After a few sprints, it became very hot and exhausting to the point that I could barely breathe. The dirt and sand from the desert floor would enter my uniform through the waist and neck areas, making it miserable to move. However, I knew that I could not quit.

The thought of a pending war was motivation enough to put forth the necessary effort to get the most out of the training because I knew that it could one day save my life. That war would come soon, and it would last longer than I imagined. After making my long dash in the desert, I was told by other Marines that were present that I was "hauling ass." I then heard that the lieutenant of 2nd platoon, Kilo Company, was impressed by the speed of my movement and accuracy of my shooting. I am sure the caffeine helped with the movement and likely helped me stay focused on the task at hand.

Training at the Twenty-Nine Palms base also included plenty of building searches. It was constantly placed in our heads that Military Operations on Urban Terrain (MOUT) was the dirtiest type of warfare, and our battalion leadership stressed the importance of preparing for it. Warfare in an urban environment typically produces large numbers of casualties on both sides. It was hoped that the more we trained and focused on this area, the fewer wounded/killed we would suffer in action. The MOUT drills would usually take place in our barracks building and would be conducted at the squad level. The training would be practiced for about two hours at a time, almost daily if the schedule allowed it.

One of the first battalion marches occurred in July of 2002 on the hot, rocky desert mountain range near the barracks buildings. Much like our assault drills, we were in full combat gear with the addition of a large rucksack, which is basically a large backpack with multiple pouches, held together by a large plastic frame. I carried about seventy pounds of gear, to include eight 30-round magazines, a large radio used for communication with higher command (battalion level), two large batteries for the radio, flak vest, helmet,

## 3. Training for War

rifle, and other military gear that would be necessary for field operations.

Our marches would last anywhere from ten to twenty miles with all aforementioned gear. Members of the Weapons Company would carry what appeared to be the heaviest load. These Marines were carrying disassembled 81mm mortars to include tubes and base plates. Other members of the Weapons Company were carrying disassembled .50 caliber machine guns, which are typically mounted on Humvees. Then you had the Javelin teams carrying large shoulder mounted rocket systems. The Weapons Company Marines had a reputation for being rather tough.

About halfway through the march, my feet began to swell up inside of my boots and my heels were beginning to feel very tender. All the weight of the gear combined with walking in the soft sand of the Twenty-Nine Palms desert began to wear on my feet. The tenderness eventually became a stinging localized pain as I continued to march with a slight limp. The irritation to my heels got so bad that I had to sit down and remove my boots midway through the hike. When I sat down, I was accompanied by a Corpsman who wanted to inspect my feet.

I then immediately removed my boots and socks. Once my socks were taken off, the Corpsman and I saw that several layers of my skin had been ripped off on both of my heels. Large patches of red tender under-skin were exposed and raw. The Corpsman then simply placed bandages over both torn heels and asked if I could continue the march. There was no way I was quitting, so I placed my bandaged feet back inside of my boots and continued the hike with the battalion. It was painful to move, but at least there was some relief to my feet with the application of the bandages.

Another part of preparing for my newly acquired assignment of radio operator was attending a one-week communications course at the Marine Corps Communications School located on the Twenty-Nine Palms base. To get trained on radio procedures, I completed the basic infantry communications classes. The instruction was rather straightforward and touched on topics of the infantry radio which was used to communicate at the company level or higher.

## 3. Training for War

Things such as maintenance, proper radio procedure, and how to properly time-sync the radio encryption were taught. Other things such as advanced communication procedures and relay stations were also brought up during the course of instruction.

The Marine Corps Air Ground Combat Center contained many shooting ranges, but the one that Marines knew was tough was the infamous Range 400. The course was a long rocky desert draw leading up to a mountain base. This range honed the infantry skills of assaulting an objective at the battalion level (approximately 1,000 men). Small arms, mortars, and heavy weapons were incorporated to overcome the imagined resistance. Heavy weapons would pin down the defenders as the infantry assaulted forward.

For riflemen, this range was somewhat dreaded because of the distance that had to be run with full gear while conducting the fire and maneuver on rocky terrain. When I ran the range for the first time, I did it in full combat gear and with my infantry radio. I remember how hot and miserable it was that afternoon. We were assaulting our objective in what appeared to be a dry riverbed. Everyone was yelling, people were trying to catch their breath from running with full gear for extending periods of time, while machine guns were blasting away nearby and in the distance. As this was going on, I was also trying my best not to trip over jagged rocks and communicate with other platoons on my radio.

As training with the battalion progressed that year, I attended one of the musters at the Twenty-Nine Palms base company area. Kilo Company's first sergeant addressed the company after our physical training session and reminded us that our battalion would be on the front lines. He also added that our unit would be the "tip of the spear" once the war in the Middle East came. From that statement alone, I knew that the plans for an invasion had already been drawn up by higher command in the Marine Corps. We were never told that we were actually going to war, but all the signs were there.

As I stood there listening to the first sergeant I recall thinking, "Well, most infantry battalions will be the 'tip of the spear' and the first to go in"; however, I did not realize at that time how right the first sergeant would be. It's amazing to think that all these people who are

## 3. Training for War

above you in rank are already deciding your destiny, for lack of a better term, and would guide which direction your life would go for the upcoming year. Their planning, or lack thereof, could be the difference between coming home in one of two ways, on your feet, or in a box. Their planning and preparation are not enough though. Training and unit discipline come into play as well.

My battalion was soon tasked with MOUT training located at Camp Pendleton. This was the same facility where MOUT was conducted during SOI. While there, the goal was to continue to familiarize Marines with fighting in an urban environment as well as developing the small unit tactics at the squad level. The battalion set up on the outskirts of the MOUT town and received classes in the morning. The battalion received the initial training brief from the cadre running the course which was comprised of the permanent core of instructors and those who were trained to assist from my battalion (mostly Lance Corporals and Corporals). We were shown a history of the battles that took place throughout recent history and what we could expect while fighting in such a three-dimensional environment. It was reinforced that casualties during an urban battle were typically higher than in any other type of terrain.

When there was free time during the training at Camp Pendleton, the newer Marines, myself included, were given the task of memorizing acronyms that pertained to infantry tactics. We would also study the nomenclature of weapons systems such as the M249 squad automatic weapon, M240G machine gun, and grenade launchers. The initial training focused primarily on room clearing, which seemed like it was practiced over and over again on "dry" runs, meaning without live ammunition/simunition rounds. Simunition rounds were ammo that could be loaded into a modified training rifle, similar to the M-16, and would discharge a small blue paintball through the barrel that would travel at a fairly high velocity. The velocity of the paintball could gain enough speed to break skin, but very rarely would cause any significant type of injury.

One of the courses contained in the MOUT training package was an assault on a building that was defended by an opposition force, role played by other Marines and MOUT instructors. Prior to the assault,

## 3. Training for War

the platoon formed along the rear wall of a nearby building in preparation for the attack. Once the order was given, my platoon ran from the cover of the building and rushed into the target location via a first-floor window. We provided the necessary cover for each other as Marines poured into the building.

Once inside, the pace became more frantic as members of the platoon provided cover on the hallways and the staircase leading to the second floor. Every room had to be cleared prior to moving upstairs. Simunition rounds were used during this training exercise and if any Marine, to include instructors, had been hit by the paintball, that person would then be out of play. My platoon would eventually assault the target building all the way toward the rooftop. At this point, there were only about three Marines left in the training exercise, myself included. The other members of the platoon had been struck by the simunition rounds from the cadre and were no longer allowed to proceed.

The remaining members of my platoon and the MOUT instructors were exchanging paintball rounds as both sides tried to gain the upper hand. The two Marines that were with me were struck by the rounds of the remaining opposition force. I flanked around the instructors to one of the other rooms while they were distracted and shot at them with what simunition ammo I had left. I was the only "surviving" member of my platoon by the time the building was deemed under our control.

The last instructor had been struck by the blue paintball as well as I; therefore, a disagreement took place about who shot who first. In the end, it was agreed that my platoon took the building. I don't think the instructors wanted to sit there to argue about the final results of the assault and wanted to proceed with the training schedule. The MOUT training that the battalion participated in would eventually be completed as the time for our eventual deployment would draw closer.

One evening, while at the Twenty-Nine Palms base, my squad leader from 1st platoon called for a squad gathering at the company barracks. He wanted to address what was expected in the combat that we knew was soon to come. He mentioned how the battalion leadership said to expect high casualties and then turned to me while

## 3. Training for War

nonchalantly saying, "Gordo, as we head into combat, the enemy will probably try to kill you first because you have the radio, and snipers will be looking for you." He then added, "You'll probably be one of the first to go." It was a very strange feeling having someone tell you so casually that you will probably be dead within a year.

I suppose that was the business we were in at that time. The business of life and death. So how does one ensure survival in this line of work? You train—and train we did. We trained so much that if there was too much down time, my squad leader would gather his group of Marines and practice fire maneuver drills on a small mountain behind the barracks. We would conduct squad rushes where we would alternate sprinting up the half sand and half rock mountain as if attacking an entrenched enemy near its peak.

The call would finally come through from higher command to be ready with all of my gear the following morning for deployment to Kuwait. It was around four in the morning when I grabbed my belongings that I needed from my house and then drove to the base. My wife Stephanie was with me as well. There was a slight feeling of excitement coupled with sadness. I was getting ready to leave for a war and the possibility of not seeing my wife or family again was very real.

Once arriving at the Twenty-Nine Palms base, I drove my car to the battalion staging area, where we waited for the buses that would eventually drive us to March Air Force Base in Riverside, California. I spent most of the early morning with my wife in our car, just lying with her and talking. My family met me on base about two hours after we arrived. My mom, stepdad, and both of my sisters were all there to see me off. When they arrived, we stood around the staging area near all of the battalion's stacked gear.

We just talked and joked around for the most part, trying to keep the mood light. My mom seemed fine until vehicles were heard coming from down the road. A long stream of white buses could then be seen headed for the battalion staging area from the main entrance of the base. I could tell my mom was trying to keep it together as the buses drew nearer. When the buses eventually arrived at the parking lot, my mom began crying. My stepfather held her to comfort her while telling her everything would be ok.

## 3. Training for War

I also told my mom that everything would be fine. "Ok, load up!" Kilo Company's gunnery sergeant loudly ordered. I then kissed and hugged my wife, then hugged each of my family members. As I grabbed my gear and was walking toward the door of the bus, my mom ran up to me to give me another big hug. I told her again that I would be ok and then walked onto the bus. As I was looking to pick my seat, I glanced out of one of the side windows facing the parking lot and could see my sisters crying with my mom.

I eventually found my seat and got situated on the bus as it began driving away from the battalion staging area. It was a strange feeling sitting there and wondering if I would see my family again. I also thought about what I might encounter on my deployment. The bus I sat in exited the base and traveled along the main highway leading into Yucca Valley, a neighboring desert town close to Joshua Tree National Park. The bus drove for several hours until arriving at March Air Force Base where we off loaded and waited in a terminal for our airplane to arrive. Once we boarded the plane, Germany would be one of our stopping points on our way to Kuwait.

# Deployment I: Operation Iraqi Freedom
*(January to June 2003)*

# 4.

# The Invasion

Arriving in Kuwait via airplane, the captain spoke on the intercom and gained the attention of all the Marines onboard. It was about four in the morning and everyone on the plane sat there quietly as the captain mentioned that he had served as a Marine some time ago. He thanked us for our service and told us he wanted to play something over the intercom before our departure. Out of the silence, I then heard the sound of a harmonica playing on the speakers and realized that the captain was playing the Marine Corps Hymn.

We all just sat there as he continued on. It was a very heartfelt moment in the plane as I felt the emotion spread without anyone saying a word. Everyone appeared to just take it in. At the end of the Hymn the captain said, "God bless you all and Semper Fi." I think he knew that not all of us would return home to our loved ones and the sense of gratitude in his voice is something that I would never forget.

Our arrival to the Middle East was at the Kuwait International Airport or "KIA" for short. It seemed slightly morbid that we were landing at an airport whose abbreviation was the exact same as the military term used for "Killed in Action." Arriving in Kuwait was somewhat of a shock for me. The culture and terrain were completely different from what I was used to in the United States.

Arabic writing was everywhere and there was sand in places as far as the eye could see. The battalion would again load onto buses which would eventually drive us to our staging area in the middle of a Kuwaiti desert. The battalion would set up camp near the border of Iraq. Marines would then place their small two-man tents on the sand in rows that aligned with their company assignment. These two-man tents would soon be replaced with larger tents that could fit several platoons within them.

When the battalion finally settled into its position in the desert, the unit would function as it would back in the United States. Physical training, grooming standards, and uniformity all had to be met to Marine Corps standard. One day during our physical training, Kilo Company, 1st squad, gathered in the open desert near our camp. Instead of a typical five-mile run, the squad leader decided to have us wrestle each other one at a time.

The squad formed a large circle as Marines would then take turns wrestling each other. The winner of the match would be the Marine who could tap the other one out and make him give up. The 1st squad leader was dominating any challenger that came his way. He was a big guy who had played some college football and barely had a neck due to his size. Every Marine from the squad that took him on had tapped out thus far.

During one of the wrestling matches, the 1st squad leader literally picked up one of the Marines by the neck and suplexed him in a way that one would see in a sports wrestling entertainment match. Once the Marine had been slammed onto the hot sand, members of the squad checked to see if he was ok. He had been slammed very hard and it looked like the air had been knocked out of him. The squad leader seemed concerned for the Marine as he was apologizing to him.

Up to that point, the squad leader had beat the entire group of Marines with the exception of me, as I had yet to wrestle him. "Come on Gordo," the squad leader said as he put out his challenge. I accepted and then stepped into the wrestling circle. It was somewhat intimidating because the Marine I was about to take on had literally just beat the entire squad and seemed pumped up to keep going. Once our match started, we fell to the sand, trying to get a dominant position for a choke hold around each other's throats. Both of us struggled to get the upper hand until I was finally able to wrap my arm around his neck while on his back.

He partially stood up while I maintained my hold as he then slammed my back onto the sand in what seemed like an attempt to break free. He struggled angrily as he tried to get out of my grip. I

## 4. The Invasion

knew not to let go because I could sense he was pissed off and he would likely go harder on me. I squeezed around his neck as hard as I could and to my surprise, he eventually tapped out to the submission shortly thereafter. As soon as he was set free, he said, "Fuck that! Let's go again!" I respectfully refused because I knew he was very upset, and I wanted to leave that match as the winner.

At the Kuwaiti camp, squad training and exercises were commonplace. The majority of my time spent at our base was with Lt Edmund and training on radio procedures. These radio procedures included calling in for medevacs, artillery/mortar rounds, air strikes, and situation reports. I would also attend quite a few briefings with Lt Edmund as the invasion of Iraq drew closer.

It seemed that sleep was a luxury in the Marine Corps. This was no different when it came to being deployed in Kuwait. On one evening, I was woken up by another Marine in the middle of the night while asleep in the tent. "Hey, it's your turn for fire watch," the Marine from my platoon stated in a loud whisper.

Still half asleep, I reached for my boots and put them on. I then grabbed my rifle and gear for the post. During fire watch, one was not allowed to sleep, and it was an obligation of the Marine on post to challenge anyone who entered the tent during the night. Fire watch shifts at that time were done in four-hour rotations. I was maybe halfway through my watch when I decided to sit down and relax.

I told myself that I was simply resting my legs and that I could keep myself awake in order to justify sitting while on post. I sat down and began reviewing notes from my field notebook. I thought, "Hey, I can simply study my field class notes to be productive. I'll stay awake, no problem." It felt like shortly after sitting down, I heard, "Hey! Get the fuck up! Who the fuck is that?!" I stood up frantically while stating my name. I had fallen asleep on shift and the Company first sergeant had suspected it. I had not challenged him when he walked through the entrance of the platoon tent.

It was very dark, and I am sure he could barely see me sitting; however, I was not walking around as expected. Therefore, the first sergeant likely figured I was asleep. "Were you fucking sleeping?! You better wake the fuck up and walk your post!" shouted the first

## Deployment I: Operation Iraqi Freedom

sergeant. "Yes, First Sergeant!" I replied while trying to act fully wake and still recovering from the initial shock of being yelled at from complete sleep.

As time in the Kuwaiti desert wore on, Kilo Company would receive their invasion briefing from inside one of the large tents at camp. It was early morning, and the plan was presented by a Marine Corps intelligence officer from division. The briefing was displayed on a large screen set up in the middle of the room. The instruction started out with battalion objectives and what the overall attack plan was for the upcoming war in Iraq. In a PowerPoint presentation, the officer pointed out the enemy units that the 1st Marine Division and our battalion would be tasked with destroying once the invasion began. Every known Iraqi tank, vehicle, and stronghold was pinpointed with GPS coordinates accompanied by satellite imagery.

The officer presenting the PowerPoint mentioned that the invasion for Iraq had been planned one year in advance. Therefore, it was obvious to me that the American government knew that Iraq would

**Marines from Kilo Company, 3rd Battalion 4th Marines, practicing room clearing within a makeshift platform in the Kuwaiti desert (March 2003).**

## 4. The Invasion

be invaded long before our arrival in Kuwait and the political posturing that led up to the war. After the overview was given, an actual computer-generated route would be shown on the briefing screen. It was a first-person point of view of the route Kilo Company would take into Iraq. The amount of detail in the planning was enormous and it was apparent that divisional headquarters wanted to ensure that every Marine knew the overall objective, as well as the specific tasks assigned to their respective units.

During the whole planning process prior to the invasion, it was continuously reinforced to us by battalion higher command that our unit would be leading from the front during the assault into Iraq. In preparation for the war, Kilo Company conducted a field exercise near the border of Iraq in the middle of the Kuwaiti desert. The focus of the training was on small unit tactics and the use of small arms. Once the training session had ended, the company formed a defensive perimeter that evening and awaited orders to return to camp.

While in the back of one of the AAVs (Amphibious Armored Vehicle), I saw large flashes of light on the other side of the border in Iraq, followed by large concussive booms that echoed throughout the desert. I mentioned to one of the other Marines that our military was bombing nearby enemy positions and that the war had already started. It made sense because the undeclared apparent artillery or air strikes gave us the element of surprise. Although the official word from higher had not been given to start the war, I had a feeling I was witnessing the preparatory bombardment that led up to the start of the Iraq conflict.

Later that week, the day would finally come in which our battalion was notified of the invasion. That morning our battalion commander had his unit gather around him as he stood above everyone on top of an American Abrams tank in the middle of a desert field near camp. He briefed us on our mission objectives and what our tactical goals were. He mentioned which Iraqi divisions we would encounter and in which cities they would be met. I was thinking, "How long will this war last? What will I see? How many of my friends and peers will die in combat? Will I die in combat?"

There were so many emotions that I was feeling at that time, mostly fear of the unknown coupled with excitement. Would the

## Deployment I: Operation Iraqi Freedom

battalion find itself in street battles like those fought in World War II, where soldiers and tanks were slugging it out in a city? Would the invasion of Baghdad turn out to be a combat "meat grinder" like that of the Battle of Stalingrad in which the invading Germany Army found itself in major urban combat against the Soviets? It was a weird feeling not knowing what was to come from the war ahead. The feeling of not knowing when I would see my family again.

Marines from my battalion conducted last-minute preparations and loaded their equipment into their respective AAVs. The Amtracks and other armored vehicles were all neatly lined up within the camp, ready for the upcoming assault into Iraq. I conducted radio checks and ensured I had all of my necessary gear. All of the Marines in the invasion were required to wear rubber MOPP (Mission Oriented Protective Posture) suits. The MOPP suit was an all-rubber one-piece outfit worn by American military personnel that was utilized as a protective barrier against chemical attack, should the Iraqi military use such measures. The military was also outfitted with rubber gloves, boots, and gas masks as additional deterrents against chemical weapons of mass destruction.

**Amphibious Armored troop carriers, also known as AAVs, lined up in preparation for the invasion of Iraq (March 2003).**

## 4. The Invasion

The invasion of Iraq would begin on March 20, 2003. There was the constant threat of a chemical attack being launched by Saddam's forces when American and allied forces set foot on Iraqi soil. During the early morning of the invasion, under the cover of darkness, there were several suspected attacks which the higher command of the 1st Marine Division thought might have been chemical in nature. Over the radios in the AAV I could hear, "Gas, gas, gas!" as the Marines and I in our track quickly donned our gas masks with rubber gloves.

The feeling was initially frantic and tense as we were all cramped in the rear of the vehicle while waiting for word about the possible gas attack. The command of "Gas, gas, gas!" over the radio seemed to be constant and the routine of throwing on your gas mask repeatedly was annoying. It was somewhat scary to say the least. We as Marines simply had to take that precaution to ensure our survival in that environment should an actual mass chemical attack present itself.

Later that morning into the invasion, the battalion set up and held

**Amphibious Armored and other American military vehicles in formation for the assault into Iraq (March 2003).**

## Deployment I: Operation Iraqi Freedom

in an open desert area just outside of Safwan Hill. From inside of the AAV, I could hear the cacophony of rockets being launched nearby. I looked out the top of the AAV and could see American rocket launcher systems firing off a huge number of munitions into the morning sky. There were maybe eight MLRS (Multiple Launch Rocket System) vehicles firing off all at once. It was amazing to see so many rockets going off into the sky with each round followed by a trail of smoke. You just knew that whoever was on the other side of that attack was not having a good day.

As the battalion moved inward into Iraq later that day, I could hear the radio come alive from the chaos that I also heard from inside the track. "Roger, we have a squad of Iraqis with machine guns moving along the embankment!" I heard a tanker voice over the radio. "We're engaging!" followed up with the tank's .50 caliber coaxial machine gun. That was the first close combat radio transmission I had heard since the invasion began. It was an uncomfortable feeling knowing that this mobile type of combat was taking place all around me and I was stuck inside a large metal vehicle.

As Kilo Company approached a town near Basra, we were ordered to dismount our AAVs and clear out the nearby buildings. The infantry needed to clear the surrounding buildings of any possible enemy fighters to help protect our advancing tanks and vehicles. As soon as we dismounted, I could immediately hear the chaotic sound of our tanks and AAVs firing off their machine guns into the neighborhood at suspected enemy positions. As I continued to run along the side of one of the tanks, I heard a Cobra attack helicopter swoop in overhead firing off into the surrounding area. I specifically remember hearing what sounded like a little girl screaming in the distance. Women could also be heard screaming as well as the frantic nature of the battle unfolded.

Marines from 1st platoon then got online and pushed inward into the small town where we believed the enemy combatants were hiding. We knew that some of the tanks had taken RPG (Rocket Propelled Grenade) fire just as the company pushed into the town. The assault into this neighborhood would eventually end without any losses on our side as the fighters fled prior to our entrance into the buildings.

## 4. The Invasion

We would make our way back to the tracks and load up for movement out of the area. The goal of the battalion was to push hard and fast northward through Iraq with the objective of reaching Baghdad quickly.

As the battalion's advance into Iraq progressed, Kilo Company AAVs pulled into an open field as we reached Basra Airport, which is located in the southern portion of Iraq. I could hear jets flying overheard and bombs being dropped in the distance. I was in the AAV with Kilo Company 1st platoon, 1st squad, accompanied by the platoon leader. We had a Scout/Sniper team attachment in the track with us as well.

Our AAV eventually drove into an open dirt area adjacent to the main landing strip. As our track pulled onto this area, I heard the sound of an incoming mortar immediately followed by a large explosion near our track. The realization set in that the Iraqis defending the airport were firing mortars at our vehicle. The initial explosion was followed by another mortar round and another. It was a helpless feeling knowing we were inside a large metal vehicle, and someone was trying to blow us up. I sat in the track silently praying very hard that the rounds would miss their target. I sat there thinking that I might die then and there with the war barely started.

The AAV kept shifting positions—not enough however to pull us out of the kill zone. The Scout/Snipers who sat with the squad in the rear of AAV became anxious. "Get the fuck out of here!" shouted one of the snipers to the platoon leader situated in the front of the AAV. "You dumb fuck! Move the fucking track!" shouted the other sniper. "That dumb fuck is going to get us killed!" The mortar fire eventually stopped after about two minutes. The enemy was either killed, forced from their position, or simply out of rounds.

Once the battalion positions were set, I, along with the Marines of 1st platoon, exited the track near the landing strip. I stepped out of the AAV and saw a surreal landscape of bomb craters with smoldering ground around the airport. I could still hear the jets overhead and I thought about the amount of damage our air power was causing among enemy troop positions. Some of the Marines pulled out their packs of cigarettes and smoked a few. Others simply stood around

## Deployment I: Operation Iraqi Freedom

while taking photos with their cameras. I took a few photographs before returning to the track after a brief period of walking around.

After the Marines returned to their respective tracks, the battalion continued its assault northward into Iraq. A few days had passed, and Kilo Company was ordered to assist with assaulting the town of Kut. The Marines of Kilo Company dismounted their AAVs and proceeded to run alongside the tanks as they reached the outskirts of the town that afternoon. Upon reaching the first set of homes, our squad came upon a locked house.

Believing the enemy had fortified the building, one Marine tossed a hand grenade through the front window. After the grenade went off, Marines proceeded to clear the house with no enemy fighters found inside. The building was empty as we moved down the road and alongside the tanks. Machine guns could be heard accompanied by main tank rounds being fired off throughout the town which added to the chaotic nature of the battle.

The company had an attachment of Marine attack helicopters overhead as we moved forward into Kut. The radio was frantic

A destroyed Iraqi armored troop carrier at Basra Airport (March 2003).

## 4. The Invasion

as platoon leaders were trying to communicate with higher command and supporting units. I could hear other Marines yelling into the radio about possible vehicle IEDs coming toward the company line followed by the concussive blast of a main tank round firing into the suspected vehicle borne IEDs. The radio was chaotic as usual with each assault into an Iraqi town.

As the battalion burst through the center of Kut, Kilo Company held on to the edge of the town prior to leaving the area. The company set up in a multi-level building as other squads cleared nearby structures. Firing could be heard from all over the city and the AAVs staged near an open field near our defensive positions. There was an enemy contingent suspected of occupying a nearby complex, maybe 100 yards away. Kilo Company needed to leave their positions and return to the tracks to continue its push deeper into Iraq. Out of fear that the suspected nearby enemy would fire on the Marines as we left our buildings, mortars were called in on the suspected enemy force.

Once the first set of mortar rounds began falling on the nearby enemy complex, Marines ran out from their occupied buildings and out onto the open courtyard to reach the tracks. The noise was chaotic as mortars fell and machine guns from the AAVs fired off to suppress the enemy positions. Kilo Company then loaded into their tracks safely and without casualties.

After clearing the town of Kut, the battalion would eventually set up in an open dirt field along an MSR (Main Supply Route) leading toward Baghdad. An artillery battery attachment was also set up in this field, likely due to an intelligence tip that an enemy unit was nearby. Lt Edmund and I dismounted our track and made our way to battalion headquarters as we walked on the soft desert dirt. On our way to headquarters, I suddenly felt my body lift violently off the ground as loud thunderous blasts of the nearby artillery unit fired off into the air. The concussions shook my entire body and took me by complete surprise.

As the week progressed and the battalion got closer to Baghdad, the unit was caught in a massive sandstorm that limited visibility to a few feet. During the daytime, the surrounding air appeared red and hazy. Due to the low visibility created by the enormous sandstorm, the

## Deployment I: Operation Iraqi Freedom

battalion had to halt into a defensive position. Marines would then exit their AAVs and set up into their security positions to protect the battalion should it come under assault. After waiting for several hours, the battalion was given the order to advance northward with Baghdad in mind.

# 5

# Diyala

The 3rd Battalion 4th Marines continued its advance toward Baghdad, fighting several skirmishes along the way with regular and irregular enemy forces. As we closed in toward the outskirts of Baghdad, the battalion held up in a small Iraqi town. It was evening, and the 1st Marine Expeditionary Force was bombing enemy positions in the distance. The night sky was filled with what appeared to be artillery rounds that gave off a red glow as they were fired off into the air. They could have been rockets; the round, however, appeared to move too slow. It looked like large fireflies all moving off in one direction upward and away from the battalion's line of defense. There were so many artillery rounds going off into the sky one would have thought that an entire Iraqi city would have been completely demolished under the bombardment.

I did notice something unusual about the suspected artillery rounds being fired off by U.S. military forces. As the projectile was lobbed off into the night sky, a few seconds later, a propellent appeared to go off from the round, sending it further into the distance. I had never seen an artillery round do that and it was quite a spectacle to see. The military was likely attempting to destroy a nearby Iraqi Army division in an open desert or palm grove area.

As the battalion got closer to Baghdad, a detachment from Kilo Company that was assigned to battalion headquarters had been ambushed alongside one of the main highways. Iraqi soldiers had fired at the Marines from bunkers dug into the dirt in a nearby palm grove and had used machine guns as well as RPGs. The detachment from Kilo Company was ordered to dismount their AAVs and assault straight into the fortified enemy position just off the side of the road.

The Marines did as they were trained and assaulted in "leapfrog" fashion. Every other Marine would provide cover fire while the others ran in short bursts toward the enemy. The Marines would alternate this pattern until the enemy was overrun. I had heard from Marines who were there that the fire fight was up close and personal. Grenades were being thrown back and forth by both sides while bunkers were being cleared out as the assault progressed. The battalion lost one Marine who belonged to the Scout/Sniper platoon. The Marine had succumbed to his injuries after the battle took place. I later overheard from the battalion commander that the skirmish in that palm grove was the most violent action he had ever seen.

The battalion would continue to push further into Iraq with Baghdad as the objective. As we drew nearer to that goal, Kilo Company would dismount from their AAVs and prepare to clear out the town of Diyala. Diyala was important to the 1st Marine Expeditionary Force because the bridge located there crossed the Tigris River and led directly into Baghdad. After dismounting the AAVs, the platoons of Kilo Company formed a skirmish line and proceeded to clear out the surrounding buildings in the area. Tanks and armored vehicles would follow in trail of one another down the main road while firing off at any suspected enemy positions.

The area near Diyala was largely green. There were palm groves that stretched along the main road leading to the bridge. As Kilo Company moved on-line, 1st platoon reached the outskirts of the river and bridge. As we approached the river, I could hear mortars being dropped on the other side of the bank where some buildings and Iraqi defenders were positioned. By the time Kilo Company had reached the river, many of the Marines were exhausted from jogging in their rubber chemical suits in full combat gear. One Marine in particular had to be treated for heat exhaustion and was given an IV by the platoon Corpsman in the rear of an AAV.

Kilo Company had already run about two miles leading from the off-load point and up to the Diyala River. Once we were able to finally reach the riverbank, 1st platoon lined up along the area in a defensive

## 5. Diyala

**Marines from Kilo Company on the assault toward the Diyala bridge (April 2003).**

position. It was maybe 100 degrees out and I was feeling it. I was sweltering in my chemical suit and was sweating profusely. The weight of the platoon radio, batteries, and ammo was beginning to wear on me as well. Most of 1st platoon were lying in a prone position and on-line looking for enemy combatants to engage on the other side of the river.

While listening to the radio, I could hear a fire mission being called in for the 81mm mortar platoon by a battalion forward observer. Within a minute, 81mm mortars came crashing into the other side of the river and onto the Iraqi defenses. The mortar explosions simply added to the chaos of Marines yelling to communicate, the multiple fires ablaze on the other side of the river, and the Abrams tanks firing their cannons/machine guns. There was also a burned-out Iraqi tank on the opposite side of the river with smoke emitting from its hull. It appeared to be a type of Russian T series tank due to the dome shaped turret.

As I lay prone on the embankment with the other Marines from 1st platoon, I could hear and see the impacts of the mortar rounds falling onto the other side of the river. The impact of the rounds began

## Deployment I: Operation Iraqi Freedom

falling from the Iraqi defensive line and gradually moved into the river toward friendly lines. I had an uneasy feeling that the mortars were being dropped in too close by our guys from Weapons Company. Shortly after, I felt the concussion of a large explosion maybe ten to fifteen yards away in the palm grove behind me. I immediately got on the radio and advised of possible short rounds from the 81mm mortar team—though the explosion could have easily been an enemy round fired onto our position. There was no direct response on the radio from Weapons Company; however, no more mortar rounds were dropped close to my position that day.

As the battle wore on during the afternoon, I began to feel very hot and lightheaded. I really began to feel the heat from the chemical suit, and I told several of the Marines around me that I was about to pass out from heat exhaustion. A few of the Marines from 1st squad helped me to remove some of my gear so that I could cool off. I was laid on my back as I opened my flak vest to air out my body. The difference was almost immediate as I could feel the excess heat dissipate.

The opposite riverbank during the battle at the Diyala bridge (April 2003).

## 5. Diyala

After pulling off the position from the edge of the river, Lt Edmund and I made our way toward the battalion command post near the Diyala bridge. We met up with a Scout/Sniper team also moving in the same direction. We were walking through a camp area where a contingent of the Iraqi military had been positioned. There was food over a small fire and some other amenities that indicated to us that the Iraqi soldiers set up there had recently fled the area mid-meal.

The fighting at the river lasted throughout the afternoon and dwindled down into the evening. Kilo Company then strengthened its defensive posture along the bank to set in for the night. Word came down from higher command that we were going to attack the other side of the bridge the following morning. Lt Edmund was advised of a stationary tank assault in which the assigned tanks/AAVs of Kilo Company would fire their .50 caliber machine guns and main tank rounds at the enemy defenses opposite of the bridge that evening. This would be a preparatory assault to soften up the enemy defenses to deter any night attack and would diminish their strength for the upcoming assault.

When the order was given for the stationary armored vehicle assault, the tanks and AAVs got online along the edge of the river. I was listening to the radio when the time came for the attack. As soon as the signal was given, every tank and most of the AAVs began firing their weapon systems. It was a furious light show coupled with the extreme noise of .50 caliber machine guns and tank cannons roaring off throughout the pitch-black river valley. Bright red tracers cut into the darkness as they crisscrossed and raced over the other side of the bridge. The stationary attack lasted for a few minutes until the firing dwindled down into silence. I wondered what could have survived such an assault.

The following morning, I asked Lt Edmund where I could grab some radio batteries in order to prepare for the upcoming bridge assault. He told me to check the AAV near the battalion command post, located several yards from the bridge. I walked over to the track and knocked on the rear metal door. The tracker inside opened the hatch and asked what I wanted. I told him that I needed some radio batteries in preparation for the attack. He appeared somewhat

## Deployment I: Operation Iraqi Freedom

annoyed that I had interrupted him and then gave me two large batteries. I thanked him and walked off to Kilo Company 1st platoon's staging area near the bridge.

As I waited with 1st platoon for the order to assault, there was a preparatory artillery barrage called in by battalion higher command. As we waited, I could hear the incoming American artillery rounds screeching overhead and impacting the opposite side of the riverbank. As the bombardment gained momentum, the impact of the rounds appeared to creep inward toward our defensive lines and staging area. Artillery rounds then began to fall into the river, shooting the water upwards with each concussive blast. I felt uncomfortable knowing the rounds were consistently coming toward our side of the river.

One round after the other impacted and continuously moved toward us. Without warning, I suddenly felt a blast of hot air rush in from behind me which pushed outward toward the river. An artillery round landed directly behind 1st platoon and into our lines. It was a nerve-wracking feeling, and the power of the blast was almost indescribable. It was frightening to say the least. It felt like a wall of super-heated air pushed me from behind followed by dust and smoke.

After reorienting myself, I could hear Marines in the command area yelling amid the chaos of what just happened. After the blast, I noticed what appeared to be a large part of an engine that landed between myself and other Marines of 1st platoon. Lt Edmund and I then ran over to the command area when we then came upon a scene of destruction. I noticed that the command AAV that was set up directly behind 1st platoon had been hit by the stray artillery round. After impacting the AAV, the explosion was apparently sent over Marines of 1st platoon. 1st platoon's staging area and the destroyed AAV were maybe ten to fifteen feet apart, separated by an eight-foot wall. The artillery round had narrowly missed an entire platoon of Marines. I likely would not be alive today had that round missed the AAV and fallen into the area where I was just standing. A situation of life and death separated by only a few feet.

Several Marines who were injured from the blast were being pulled away from the area of impact. I walked around to the rear of the command AAV and saw something that I will never forget. Blood

## 5. Diyala

covered the floor of the rear track door, and the surrounding gear was covered in bits of flesh. On one of the Kevlar helmets, I saw a part of one of the deceased Marine's brains on top of it. It was a gruesome and saddening sight.

I also observed a Corpsman working on one of the trackers who had been injured by the blast; however, the tracker did not make it through. Two Marines whom I had just seen and one of whom I had just spoken to were killed by an incoming artillery round. I was shaken up to say the least by what just happened. I almost lost my life and just witnessed my first look at American war dead. Many other injured Marines were being hauled away, to include 1st platoon's 1st squad leader. He was medevac'd out of the area shortly thereafter.

I accompanied Lt Edmund as he walked around looking for the other trackers near the riverbank amongst the buildings. One of the trackers frantically walked in our direction toward the destroyed AAV. The Marine was asking what happened with a worried look in his eyes. Lt Edmund then put his hand out and shook the Marine's hand while saying, "I'm so sorry." The tracker immediately knew his friends had just been killed. Tears began rolling down his cheeks as he stood there looking toward the ground in apparent disbelief. He did not say a word.

Once 1st platoon was able to regather itself, Marines set up again for the upcoming assault across the Diyala bridge. There was a group of Marine Corps engineers attached to the company that would repair the hole in the pedestrian crossing. The plan was for the engineers to lay down metal planks over the large hole, so that the rest of the Marines could run across on foot. The 1st squad of the 1st platoon was to provide cover fire for the engineers as they repaired the crossing, as well as provide cover for the remainder of the platoon running across the bridge.

In preparation for the assault, tanks and AAVs lined up along the edge of the riverbank. The attack would start with the firing of the tanks and AAVs. Kilo Company waited anxiously for the preparatory fire to begin which would signal the crossing. Once the order was given over the radio, the silence of that morning was interrupted by the tremendous noise of machine gun fire coupled with tanks firing

## Deployment I: Operation Iraqi Freedom

their cannons. I immediately ran toward the bridge with 1st squad accompanied by the engineer attachment. We ran as fast as we could until we reached the hole in the pedestrian crossing about halfway on the bridge. A machine gunner attached to the squad was firing at the hip into the other side of the embankment toward suspected enemy positions.

I immediately found cover near one of the metal supporting beams on the bridge and fired into the thick brush on the opposite side of the river. The Marines provided steady rifle and machine gun cover as the engineers frantically placed the beams over the hole. The noise of the firing from the Marines was chaotic and provided me with a rush of adrenaline. It took the engineers about a minute to cover the damaged area, at which time they called for the remainder of 1st platoon to cross over the bridge. Media photographers were mixed in with us as 1st squad provided cover fire as the rest of 1st platoon approached. They were taking photos as Marines ran across the bridge. The event leading up to and during the bridge battle was well covered by the *Wall Street Journal*.

I could hear the engineers yelling, "Let's go, let's go!" as Marines poured across the bridge. The aim was to get across quickly and establish a foothold on the opposite side. As we ran as fast as possible, we rushed past a dead Iraqi man lying on the foot path. 1st squad was able to reach the opposite set of buildings with relative ease. We were amongst the first set of Marines to officially enter Baghdad during the invasion.

1st squad and I then cleared the nearby buildings overlooking the bridge to eliminate the possibility of ambush on the remaining Marines crossing. The structure was full of bullet holes and partially destroyed. 1st squad and I then cleared about one block northward away from the bridge. There I saw a parked truck on the road with the driver slumped over on the steering wheel. The driver had been shot in the face by our forces, likely by one of our snipers. He was probably killed because he failed to yield to warning shots. There was always the possibility of the driver blowing up the bridge with a vehicle laden with explosives.

After clearing the northbound street, 1st platoon regrouped and

## 5. Diyala

was redirected to the intersection northwest of the bridge. The order was to clear the westward road through the neighborhood along with the adjacent buildings. As 1st platoon moved toward the intersection, we jogged along the partially destroyed road in which some areas of the neighborhood were emitting smoke. About one block down the road, we traveled past a dead Iraqi body lying face down near the sidewalk. It appeared to be a male and his body was partially burned. It looked as if he ran out of a nearby burned-out vehicle while on fire and was likely shot up by machine gun rounds. Or he simply burned to death.

The chaos and reality of the battle was really beginning to set in. I had seen two dead Americans and several deceased Iraqis. It was not a good feeling being surrounded by so much death and destruction. Once 1st platoon reached its objective, we set up a defensive line to prohibit any vehicle borne IEDs or enemy troop movement through the area. Shortly after the line was set, an Iraqi man began walking toward our positions from half a block away. He was walking from a nearby neighborhood and Marines were shouting at him to stop; however, he slowly kept moving toward us in a stoic manner.

The Iraqi man showed no emotion as he continued walking toward the defensive line. Marines then fired warning shots at him. The rounds impacted the wall near him on the sidewalk and close to his head; however, the man simply walked off into a nearby building. I was amazed at what little emotion he showed, especially while being shot at. Marines were wary of suicide bomber attacks and would not take any chances with their lives. A part of me was relieved he did not die; however, had he been strapped with an explosive vest, there would have been no hesitation on my part to protect my fellow Marines.

As we held the line, a vehicle came speeding down the road toward our position. Marine snipers from the rooftops located to our rear, on the opposite side of the river, could be heard shooting at the car. I overheard on the radio that the snipers were attempting to shoot out the engine of the oncoming vehicle. The speeding car came within fifty yards of our lines as we fired off our rifles and machine guns. The car stopped and the driver immediately jumped out of the driver's seat and was shot down by Marine fire. I had never seen anything like it.

## Deployment I: Operation Iraqi Freedom

The Iraqi man oddly spun around as he was riddled with bullets and collapsed onto the street where he died.

I was shocked at what I saw. The death that day just continued as I witnessed a human being shot dead in front of me. Another vehicle came down the road toward our position shortly after. This time it was a van. The van, much like the other vehicle, traveled toward our line and did not stop. Believing that it might be carrying an IED, we fired into the van to stop it. I could hear the Kilo Company's executive officer yelling into the radio, "Stop shooting at the fucking cars, goddamn it!" I told Lt Edmund that higher command wanted us to stop shooting at the vehicles; however, during the noise and chaos of the situation, Marines continued to fire.

I again shouted to Lt Edmund that higher was telling us not to shoot at the vehicles. It did not matter. It seemed like there was simply too much yelling and shooting going on for any word to get effectively passed around to the troops. The risk of a car bomb coming into friendly lines was real and the Marines from 1st platoon were not taking any chances. I suppose from the safety of a rooftop about 200 yards across the river and behind our lines, it was easier for command to order the Marines not to fire into the oncoming vehicles as they drove toward us. I did not like the idea of shooting anyone; however, I also did not like the idea of being blown up along with my platoon members. Vehicle IEDs were a very real possibility and higher command had advised us that fighting in Baghdad would be fierce.

# 6

# Baghdad

We were eventually ordered to move out from our defensive posture and push northward, approximately two blocks into the neighborhood. 1st platoon and I stopped near a small building surrounded by a palm grove adjacent to the main street leading toward Baghdad. As we came upon the small building, we noticed that the large steel door leading into the structure was locked. We were able to eventually unlock it and were somewhat surprised by what we found inside. The building contained about a hundred AK rifles along with other Iraqi military equipment such as compasses, binoculars, and gas masks.

Several Marines from 1st platoon were tasked with pulling out the rifles and laying them out onto the ground so that they could be destroyed. The firearms were laid out in a linear pattern so that one of the AAVs attached to Kilo Company could run them over and render them useless, should the enemy backtrack to their cache. After the rifles had been pulled out, I made sure to grab some Iraqi military equipment as war souvenirs. I retrieved a gas mask, compass, and a set of binoculars. Some of the other Marines grabbed war souvenirs as well.

It was almost excruciating to watch as the AAV ran over so many AK rifles in good condition. So many decent firearms were crushed in one simple drive over by an armored track troop carrier. However, I knew it was for the better because the company did not want to be bogged down loading and transporting so many weapons. At this time, I heard the sound of one of the SAW machine guns fire off nearby. It was another Marine from 1st squad firing down one of the side streets. "I just saw several guys running! I got them!" said the Marine. He then told me that he had seen an enemy contingent running and had shot them down with his machine gun.

After discovering the enemy weapons cache, Kilo Company regrouped and headed for the heart of Baghdad. Eventually the company came upon a palm grove after several blocks of traveling. It was believed that enemy fighters could be hidden within the grove just as they were when Kilo Company 3rd platoon was ambushed from one just before reaching the Diyala River. The AAVs and tanks lined up in formation just outside of the vegetated area to conduct a reconnaissance by fire. The tracks' and tanks' .50 caliber machine guns rattled off into the palm grove, raking any possible enemy positions. The grenade rounds launched from the tracks' Mk 19 machine guns were also heard as they were lobbed and impacted the ground about thirty yards away.

After the reconnaissance by fire, we dismounted from our AAVs and formed a skirmish line alongside the tracks just outside of the palm grove. The order to push forward was then given as we walked in unison. Marines would fire into any nearby buildings or vegetated areas that looked like they were concealing enemy positions. The area I walked along was adjacent to a small set of buildings near the palm grove. One of the squad leaders from 2nd platoon Kilo Company was about ten feet in front of me when I shot into a second story window that could have been used as a firing position.

The squad leader from 2nd platoon then angrily turned around and yelled, "You know I'm right here, right?!" "Yeah, I saw you." I replied. My muzzle direction was nowhere near him and had been pointed upward at the building window I just shot at. He likely heard the shot and assumed I was firing past him into the palm grove. We pushed into the palm grove until higher command was satisfied that there were no enemy combatants in the immediate area. When the grove was deemed secure, we loaded back into our respective AAVs and continued the push into Baghdad.

The order to exit our tracks and clear nearby buildings seemed to be repeated in a short span of time as we searched neighborhoods on the outer portion of the city. If there was any suspicion of an enemy force nearby, we would clear out the structures for the armor attached to the company. It was a tiresome ordeal because of the heat and full

## 6. Baghdad

combat gear we were wearing. When the buildings were cleared, the Iraqi military usually had already fled the area and was nowhere to be found. We would find ditched Republican Guard uniforms and berets on the floor where the enemy troops had left them.

"Dismount!" was overheard yet again on the AAV radio as we then exited our vehicles to provide security for the armor as we moved into the city of Baghdad. It was still very hot as we formed along both sidewalks in the Iraqi neighborhood adjacent to our tanks/tracks on the roadway. We kept pace with the tanks by running alongside them from a reasonable distance. We were still in full combat gear, this time without the MOPP suits, and the sense of urgency to get to the center of the city could be felt. We jogged alongside the armored vehicles for about ten minutes when I heard Kilo Company's commander yelling "Keep going! Don't stop!" from atop his command AAV. We continued to jog in the mid-day heat as I heard Marines trying to catch their breath amid the noise of shooting and tank engines, as I was. It was just a "keep going and don't stop until we get to the center of the city" kind of blitz.

As Kilo Company approached the center of Baghdad, we were bypassing Iraqi citizens; however, something was different. The women there were not dressed in the garb that Americans may typically associate with Iraqi women. Many of them dressed no differently from American women, wearing shirts and tight jean pants. Many of the Iraqi men were dressed in western clothing as well. None of the citizens in this particular area seemed upset at our presence and there was no resistance.

We eventually entered the heart of Baghdad shortly thereafter, and our company made its way into an Iraqi Christian neighborhood. This was apparently a designated rallying point for Kilo Company which was likely a pre-planned staging site before the invasion as it was a friendly area. The Iraqi citizens in the neighborhood appeared genuinely happy to see us. Many Iraqi men were shaking our hands and children were eager to talk to us. The company eventually set up the command post in a park within the Christian neighborhood. A perimeter was then set, and posts were designated by the company commander.

# Deployment I: Operation Iraqi Freedom

**Here I am posing on a Baghdad rooftop after recently entering the city (April 2003).**

Later that night, Lt Edmund and I were invited by an Iraqi man into his home for dinner. He spoke decent English. We were then immediately shown the dining room area where food was already set out. I don't recall exactly what was served that evening other than eating some pickled olives and what I believe may have been lamb. The Iraqi man and his wife were very nice. He then offered Lt Edmund and me an Iraqi made cigarette which we both agreed to take. We sat there in his kitchen while smoking, which was a nice break from the continuous combat and constant movement that had recently taken place. The Iraqi man spoke to Lt Edmund about the invasion as I sat there in the dining area listening to the platoon radio.

After eating, Lt Edmund and I made our way back to where 1st platoon had set up for the night within a nearby church compound. Once there, we entered the building and took off our gear so that we could relax. I eventually made my way outside to the front of the building where Iraqi nuns were pouring coffee for the Marines. The hospitality was surprising, and the nuns also brought out some flat bread. The flat bread tasted very good, especially after eating MRE's for almost two weeks straight.

The following morning, we received word that a large Iraqi crowd was trying to force its way into a large Baghdad bank, and we were being sent out for crowd control. The bank was located a few blocks away from our compound and once we arrived, it was largely a chaotic

## 6. Baghdad

scene. The members of the Iraqi crowd were yelling and trying to force their way into the main entrance of the bank. My platoon, along with members of the attached AAVs, forced our way past the crowd and into the building. We stood online near the main entrance while forcing people back. Other Marines from my platoon forced out Iraqis who were already inside the bank and attempting to loot the facility at floor level. Smoke could be seen coming from the vault located downstairs as Marines rushed past the remaining Iraqis outside.

I also saw Marines going downstairs to clear the vault from any possible looters. I, along with other Marines, kept back the angry Iraqi crowd as we tried to bring order to the situation. A few minutes had passed when I looked behind me toward the stairs leading to the vault. I then saw 2nd platoon's 2nd squad leader stumbling his way back to floor level from the vault stairs, as he then fell onto the Marine nearest him. He had been wearing his gas mask to protect himself; however, the filter on the mask apparently did not completely protect him against smoke inhalation.

The 2nd squad leader was eventually laid onto the floor as one of the Corpsman did what he could to get a response from him. It did not take long for the oxygen deprived Marine to regain his consciousness. There was a sense of relief when he woke up. Several other Marines who had gone downstairs into the vault area had also passed out as other Marines tended to them. All the Marines who passed out from the smoke inhalation were treated and eventually came to without serious injury.

The bank would eventually become secured by American forces to prevent further looting. When we returned to the company command area, we relaxed and ate some food. There was some down time and word was passed that one of the reporters from the *San Francisco Chronicle* was allowing Marines to use his satellite phone to call home. I, along with other Marines, made our way to the reporter and anxiously waited in line to call our families back in the United States. When my turn came, the reporter looked at me and asked how old I was. I told him nineteen and his response was that I looked like I was twelve.

The reporter's comment was mildly interesting as I knew he was a

## Deployment I: Operation Iraqi Freedom

former active-duty Marine, though he did not serve in direct combat. He had reported on other conflicts, and I recall a comment he made about the Marines fighting in the invasion of Iraq. I believe he mentioned that he had seen more combat than them because of where he had been during his past reporting. Seeing and reporting on combat is different from participating in it. Of course, he is still in harm's way; however, I assume he was not a direct target for enemy troops as he is not armed and is watching the combat from the sidelines. He is not ordered to assault a position or enter a building possibly full of armed combatants.

When I was able to use the satellite phone, I called my mom. She was very excited to hear my voice, as I was to hear hers. She told me that she was proud of me and could not wait until I came home. I had to keep the call brief as other Marines were awaiting their turn. I then told her that I loved her and would see her soon.

My battalion would remain in Baghdad for about another week or two until we were replaced by an Army unit. The battalion would then make its way to a staging area on the outskirts of Baghdad. This area was a large open desert and there were almost no buildings in sight. While there, it appeared as if fires in the distance would spontaneously arise as smoke was continuously forming in several different directions. Iraq seemed to have its own odor as well. It was not necessarily good or bad; however, the country did have its own distinct aroma. The battalion stayed in this position for a few days.

On one afternoon, Kilo Company 2nd platoon's staff sergeant called for a classroom circle. It was common for the company leadership to give what were called "hip pocket" classes or briefings to stave off boredom or to fill the Marines' free time. I don't exactly recall what was briefed, but it related to security posts for the battalion staging area and where the battalion would go next in Iraq before we headed back to the United States. I think the Marines, including myself, were tired of the briefings and I would expect many had their minds on returning home. I know I did, and the vibe was felt throughout the platoon, if not the entire battalion.

About five minutes into the brief, the staff sergeant suddenly stopped talking as his face turned from relaxed to serious. He then

## 6. Baghdad

suddenly stated, "Look! I know you guys don't give a fuck about what I have to say right now, and you all want to go home! I want to go home too! Until then, pay the fuck attention and let's get through this together!" What he said was unexpected; however, the vibe amongst the Marines sitting in on the briefing remained the same. I know I was tired and thinking of home.

The battalion would eventually move out of its position in the open desert and would move to a more secure location. The last two weeks in Iraq were boring to say the least. We were anxious to return home and our living quarters for the remaining time in country were limited to an old Iraqi military compound, no bigger than about two acres. Attending the battalion chaplain's services every Sunday did alleviate some of the anxiousness I felt at that time. It felt good to be in that positive environment and seeing other Marines get along as opposed to fighting with each other over the petty disputes that would sometimes arise.

I would try to pass the time at the compound by working out, reading, or listening to the CD player that my family sent me. There was really not much else to do other than to wait for the order to go home. The tension while waiting to get back to the United States would build up and one day, while walking to my tent, another Marine from 1st platoon made a comment to me. I don't recall exactly what was said, but I made a remark back to him. He then asked if I "...wanted to go!" I simply walked up to him, and we immediately started to wrestle as we fell over the lined up two-man tents. We were not mad at each other, but it was a good way to stave off some of the boredom.

When the order came down that the battalion would soon be leaving the compound, the feeling of excitement was overwhelming. We were one step closer to going home and we would no longer have to stay in Iraq much longer. By leaving the former Iraqi military grounds, there was the promise of better food, amenities, and shelter. When battalion left the compound, we eventually returned to Kuwait. There we would fly out of Kuwaiti International Airport and subsequently return to the United States.

The flight home would make stops in Germany, Maryland, and then finally to March Air Force base. From there, we would eventually

## Deployment I: Operation Iraqi Freedom

board the buses that would take us back to the Marine Corps Air Ground Combat Center. There was a feeling of elation. For me, I thought the war was over and that I would never have to return to Iraq. As the buses got closer to the Marine Twenty-Nine Palms base, it seemed as if everyone on the bus could barely contain their excitement.

The buses we were in then drove toward the north gym on the base. As the buses slowly, but surely trudged up the hill, we could see our family and friends waiting in the parking lot. They were holding up signs and were obviously excited at the sight of our arrival. We could hear everyone shouting and cheering as we pulled into the off-load area. Once the buses stopped, we exited as quickly as we could to greet our loved ones. I was then immediately met by my family. My mother, stepfather, and sisters were there as I gave my mom the biggest hug possible. We held each other as she cried, likely from the thought that she might not have seen me again. Little did she know how close that thought came to becoming a reality.

I then hugged the rest of my family members. I had never felt that much excitement and joy up to that point in my life. The weather that day was perfect with clear skies. Words almost can't describe how I felt. I survived the war and was greeted by those that I loved the most. I also had a huge sense of accomplishment. At that time, I thought the war was completely over and that the Army would complete sustainment operations in Iraq to help stabilize the country. With all of the excitement and happiness aside, I also felt sad because my wife was not there to greet me. She was still in Iraq, and I missed her a lot.

As months went by after returning home, I would speak to Stephanie over the phone every chance I got. I loved hearing her voice. It was just such a relief to know that she was ok. During one of our phone calls, I found out that she had volunteered for the deployment with her unit to her Iraq. When I asked her why, she stated that she would be closer to me. This irritated me because she would have been home had she not volunteered to go overseas. This would eventually lead to resentment and other issues within our marriage.

My return home was not without its time of personal reflection on what I had experienced during the invasion of Iraq. I had almost

## 6. Baghdad

died, and I witnessed Americans, as well as Iraqis, lose their lives. I knew I was affected by the piece of combat that I had gone through. Many times, when no one was around, I would tear up at the thought of seeing the two American trackers torn apart by an artillery round or the thought of seeing Marine bullets rip into some Iraqi citizens who were likely fleeing the chaos around them. I was young and those experiences were all new to me.

# 7

# Scout/Sniper Platoon

Information came down from battalion command that the Scout/Sniper platoon would be having their indoctrination or "indoc" in the spring of 2003. Most of the guys in the Scout/Sniper platoon were in their last year of enlistment and were leaving the Marine Corps in a few months. The indoctrination would include a physical fitness test, endurance exercises, and an interview by members of the platoon. For the start of the tryouts, there was a list of items to bring on the first day of the indoc. If you did not have the items requested by the members of the platoon, you would be excused and sent back to your line company.

The 3rd Battalion 4th Marines Scout/Sniper platoon consisted of veteran snipers who all just recently served in Operation Iraqi Freedom. I had interacted with a few of the Scout/Sniper members during my time in Iraq and looked up to them. They appeared to be very professional; however, they did not adhere to the typical gung-ho Marine attitude. The Scout/Sniper platoon consisted mainly of HOGs or in other words "Hunter of Gunmen," school trained Scout/Snipers who completed the course that took place at Camp Pendleton, California. There was only one Scout/Sniper in the platoon that I overheard was not school trained; however, I respected him nonetheless.

A few days prior to the indoc, I and other members of Kilo Company were returning our weapons to the armory at the Twenty-Nine Palms base after a training exercise. I had signed up for the indoc and apparently the battalion armorer got word that I was trying out. As I was turning in my M-16 at the armory gate, the Marine said, "I heard you were trying out for the sniper platoon." I simply told him yes. His

## 7. Scout/Sniper Platoon

response was, "You're not going to make it." I just looked at him and laughed without saying a word.

When the time for the Scout/Sniper indoc came, Marines who wanted to try out would meet early in the morning on base for the start of the process. The physical fitness test started at around 3:00 a.m. near the base soccer field. There were probably around forty Marines, including myself, that showed up for the tryouts. I felt some anxiety and nervousness before the initial test. What was the day going to be like? How tough was this indoctrination?

The physical fitness test started with the usual three-mile run, followed by pull-ups and sit-ups. It was very cold and by the last mile I ran I was somewhat exhausted while trying to catch my breath. When the time came for the pull-ups, I believe I did around fifteen to twenty repetitions. I could hear the Scout/Snipers yelling at Marines to use proper form and to lock out their elbows to get the count for the pull-up. I maxed out on the sit-ups at 100 crunches. Some members of the platoon would do the exercises with us and would always demand for the Marines to put forth their best effort.

It was about 8:00 a.m. when the time came for a three-mile sandbag run. The run would take place in full utility uniform and boots. Each Marine participating was given a sandbag filled with dirt to place into their rucksacks. As we started at a steady jog, could feel the weight of the sandbag on my shoulders and knew it was going to be a rather painful experience. The run would start from our battalion area parking lot which would then lead into the mountains that butted against the eastern portion of the base. I could immediately feel a large amount of pressure on my shoulders and wondered how much I might suffer during the exercise.

After conducting the sandbag run, the Marines who remained and did not quit were ordered to get into platoon formation at the battalion parking lot. We immediately grounded the sand-filled packs and one Marine from Kilo Company who happened to be nearby told me, "I don't know how you are doing it." The Marine appeared to appreciate what I was going through and was likely glad it was not him enduring the apparent hazing. I thanked him and continued with the indoctrination. The number of Marines who tried out for the Scout/

# Deployment I: Operation Iraqi Freedom

Sniper platoon had dwindled down that day by more than half. The physical effort that was required that morning was apparently too much for some of the Marines and they simply quit the process.

Later in the week, Marines who were left from the tryouts had to be interviewed by members of the Scout/Sniper platoon. When my turn came, I had to stand in front of the Scout/Snipers who were sitting down near a large table in one of the battalion's briefing rooms. They asked why I wanted to be a member and what I had done to prepare to be there. I was nervous; however, I answered their questions with relative ease. One of the platoon members present was Sgt James Delgadio. He would go on to be the first Marine Corps Special Operations sniper instructor and a military author. The level of quality that the Scout/Snipers possessed could not be overstated. These guys were professionals, and they knew it. A military novelist by the name of Jeff Cameron had also been a member of the 3rd Battalion 4th Marines Scout/Sniper platoon; however, I believe he retired from the Marine Corps by the end of Operation Iraqi Freedom.

The Marines who were left over from the initial indoc phase that day would continue to be tested with observation, knowledge, and physical fitness exercises throughout the upcoming weeks. These exercises would then be intermittently interrupted by platoon runs to the top of the hills on base or other areas within the combat center designated by the HOGs. A large focus of the training was placed on testing our memory skills and recalling verbatim the definitions of Scout/Sniper terms. Some of the memory training would consist of conducting physical training interrupted by the HOGs running the inductees to a certain area in which multiple items were laid out for us to memorize. The items would only be visible to us for a short amount of time before we were run off to another area for more physical training. The physical training would then be interrupted by recalling and writing down the name, size, shape, and color of the items we had previously viewed on our pocket notebooks or folders.

One morning, the Marines who had made it through the indoc phase with the Scout/Sniper platoon were ordered to meet at the on-base swimming pool for some exercises. The platoon would conduct a "run-swim-run" drill in which we would conduct swimming

## 7. Scout/Sniper Platoon

exercises followed by a run around the base, probably about a mile, which was followed up by more swimming. The physical training almost seemed relentless and a few more Marines would drop out from the platoon to return to their respective companies.

A few weeks after the start of the Scout/Sniper indoc, I saw the battalion armorer when retrieving the M-40 sniper rifle from the armory. I had been accepted into the platoon and recalled what the armorer had said to me about trying out for the unit. He would not look me in the eye. I was one of the very few Marines that had made it past the initial phase of the indoc and I believe he knew it. Regardless, I did not hold a grudge and would continue to focus on what was being taught by the HOGs.

We were to receive more classroom instruction from the Scout/Snipers at the base briefing center the following month. I was studying material given to me by members of the platoon, just outside of the classroom building, when I was told by one of the HOGs to go inside for the period of instruction. This particular Scout/Sniper, Sgt Danner, was a very professional guy and had been the honor graduate for his class when he completed Scout/Sniper school. I replied, "Yes, Sergeant" just before entering the building. I had a huge amount of respect for him and maybe he could tell by the way I responded. "Hey look, I am no better than you or anyone," he said. "You can relax and talk to me like a normal person."

The training received by the HOGs in the 3rd Battalion 4th Marines Scout/Sniper platoon seemed constant. If we weren't doing memory drills, it was observation training. If we weren't in the classroom receiving instruction, it would be running around the base with intermittent push-ups, pull-ups, and sit-ups. In our free time, we were ordered to memorize Scout/Sniper terms verbatim or write a fifty-page order over the weekend.

As my time in the Scout/Sniper platoon progressed into the winter of 2003, the few remaining new guys in the group, to include myself, went with the battalion to receive mountain warfare training in Bridgeport, California. This area was the Marine Corps' training center in mountainous terrain. There, Marines honed patrolling techniques, rock climbing, and other skills pertaining to that environment.

## Deployment I: Operation Iraqi Freedom

The platoon would receive Scout/Sniper training from the instructors on base in the form of the high angle package. The high angle package would be given to the HOGs of the platoon while the new guys would tag along for the instruction, the only difference being the intermittent workouts (some may call it hazing) with additional training for good measure.

Once arriving at the Marine Corps Mountain Warfare Training Center, the Marines settled into the barracks on base. Our barracks area was a small quonset hut which just happened to be near the base of a large mountain. At this time, there were only six remaining Marines who had initially tried out for the platoon, myself included. It was a mixture of Marines from India, Kilo, and Weapons Company.

The following day, as the platoon got in line for afternoon chow at the base cafeteria, one of the HOGs asked me how I thought the training would be that day. He was a tall Japanese-American guy, in his early twenties. I simply told him that I did not know. His response was, "It's going to be fucking gay, that's what it is going to be!" Then he went on to say how the battalion level training was stupid and ineffective. The Scout/Sniper platoon members did not seem to care about what the battalion had to offer as far as training was concerned and they seemed to have a lack of respect for a large portion of its leadership.

Later that evening, the Chief Scout of the platoon had the group throw on their ghillie suits for our physical training session. The ghillie suit is a military BDU uniform laced with netting on the back side, used for applying vegetation with the aim of blending into the surrounding environment. We then grabbed our packs and rifles as we got in formation on the dirt lot outside of our barracks. The Chief Scout then ran the group toward the mountain behind the barracks at which time we were accompanied by several other Scout/Snipers from the platoon. We ran until we were told to come to a halt near a muddy marsh. Sweaty and slightly out of breath from the run, we were then told to drop our gear. "Get in and cover every inch of that suit in mud!" demanded the Chief Scout. "You need to blend into your surroundings."

After covering ourselves in mud, we were forced to run with our packs and gear up the nearby mountain. The weight of the mud mixed into the fibers of the ghillie suit was felt and made the run that much more uncomfortable. We ran until we were halfway up the mountain along a dirt road. The group was then told to get on the ground and start doing push-ups. At this time, I suddenly heard cadence being sung down the road we just came from.

A platoon from Kilo Company appeared shortly thereafter and was running in their very clean PT clothing while continuing to shout their cadence. The Chief Scout then told our group to immediately stand up. He then told us to turn our backs on the platoon as they were approaching. "Turn around and face me, don't even fucking look at them!" snarled the Chief Scout as the platoon passed us.

Our group would eventually run again after the push-ups, and we would come to a stop in the middle of a forest area for a training brief. The platoon sat around the Scout/Sniper platoon leader as he gave his briefing regarding the training that would take place that evening. He was a tall and lanky Caucasian male, in his early thirties. As the platoon leader continued talking, one of the Scout/Snipers started laughing. I could tell that the sniper had very little respect for him, and his laughing was a clear indication of that. "What is so funny?" the platoon leader asked. The sniper continued to laugh while simultaneously saying, "I don't know" as he stared directly at him. The platoon leader then gave the sniper an annoyed look while continuing to brief the unit where he had left off.

The following day, the PIGs from the Scout/Sniper platoon were tasked with "stalking" that afternoon. The training would take place on a nearby mountain side which had a gradual slope. We were ordered to put on our ghillie suits and were given a class on the basics of stalking for Scout/Sniper school. There was an emphasis on slow and deliberate movements with the idea of only using fresh vegetation from the surrounding area so that we were able to continuously blend in with our environment. The stalking course that day seemed long and gritty. We had to low crawl in our ghillie suits for hundreds of yards all while covered in organic material in the midday sun.

Later that evening, the platoon had some down time in the barracks at Bridgeport. One of the larger built Scout/Snipers then

## Deployment I: Operation Iraqi Freedom

challenged some of the PIGs to a wrestling match in which whoever tapped the other one out first would lose the fight. The Scout/Sniper then challenged one of the PIGs directly, and he accepted. Both started wrestling as the other tried to gain the upper hand in the fight. The PIG was eventually able to get on the back of the larger Scout/Sniper and was able to sink in a choke hold around his neck. Both were on the ground as the HOG desperately tried to break free from the hold that restricted his breathing. The HOG finally tapped out, which came as a surprise to me. The HOG was probably twice the size of the other Marine.

Near the end of the mountain training that had gone on for about two weeks, the lead sniper instructor at Bridgeport, who led the "High Angle Package," invited the platoon over to his house for a barbeque. The platoon then shuttled over to the instructor's house and once we arrived, we were told by the instructor that we as new guys could not consume alcohol. When we settled in at the house, the HOGs, with the exception of the PIGs, began drinking beer. The sniper instructor then crouched over the PIGs as we sat on a bench in the backyard of his home. He asked why we were not drinking while using a nerdy mocking tone. We simply replied that we were specifically told not to drink; however, I'm sure he already forgot because he was apparently drunk. He kept asking us if we wanted a beer and we all respectfully refused with the exception of one PIG.

Within about two months of being in the Scout/Sniper platoon, I was the only member of the original group of Marines who had tried out. The other PIGs had quit and returned to their line companies within the battalion. Almost all of the original HOGs had left the Marine Corps as well. During the two months, a Recon Marine by the name of Sgt Joseph and another Scout/Sniper named Sgt Wright joined the platoon. Sgt Shane, who had been part of a 7th Marines Scout/Sniper platoon, joined the unit as well.

The only Marines left were the platoon leader, platoon staff sergeant, Sgt Joseph (Chief Scout), Sgt Wright, Sgt Shane and me. Without anybody else to focus on, I was given the opportunity to receive high-quality training from an elite group of Marines. Given that, I had plenty of free time to go to the gym to lift weights and swim at the base

## 7. Scout/Sniper Platoon

pool on every lunch break. I must admit that life at that time was not too bad; however, this may have lasted for only about two months.

The Scout/Sniper platoon leader was impressed with my performance so far with the unit. One morning while at battalion headquarters, he pulled me aside into the Scout/Sniper office and told me that I was one of the best Marines he had ever seen. He then proceeded to tell me to be a leader and to carry on with the platoon. Sgt Joseph was present in the office and was standing by silently. It felt pretty good to hear him tell me that, but then again, I knew it was his job to keep me motivated to stay with the platoon.

After speaking with the platoon leader, I stepped out of the office, and was followed out by Sgt Joseph. He then pulled me aside and told me that he was the Chief Scout for the platoon; therefore, he was in charge. I'm not sure if he felt threatened by what the platoon leader told me or if he just wanted to keep me grounded to ensure I knew my place in the unit. Either way, I thought it was arrogant of him to take the time to pull me aside and tell me that he was in charge. For me, it was simply an honor to be part of the group and it was not my intention to push anyone aside or to promote without earning it first.

As my time with the Scout/Sniper platoon progressed, the 3rd Battalion 4th Marines would prepare to participate in a large, combined arms exercise that would be positioned at a small area within the Marine Corps Air Ground Combat Center. This area was known as Camp Wilson and there our unit would conduct preparations for the upcoming training. Once arriving, gear and equipment had to be shuttled into the battalion staging area for the operation. At that time, I was tasked with grabbing the platoon's water jugs from our Humvees.

While at Camp Wilson, I had brought two empty five-gallon water drums into the bathroom with me. I set them aside about a foot behind me as I then began to pee in the urinal. A captain from the battalion was peeing in a nearby urinal and asked, "Are those water jugs? Get that shit out of here, we drink water out of those!" I simply replied, "Yes, sir," and proceeded to take the jugs out of the bathroom. It's not like I peed directly into the jugs or had them open; however, I recognized his point.

## Deployment I: Operation Iraqi Freedom

I eventually made my way back to the company quonset hut where the Scout/Sniper platoon leader and the sergeants were going over plans for the upcoming training exercise. The exercise would include a coordinated battalion effort in a nearby mountain range at the Marine Corps Air Ground Combat Center that would include offensive and defensive actions. As I was reviewing the plans, I was listening to my headphones while reading the order of operations. "Hey, take those off while you read that! How are you supposed to concentrate on what you are going over?" Sgt Shane demanded. I advised him that I was reading the plans just fine and that the headphones were not a distraction. He insisted that I take them off; therefore, I complied.

Later that evening, our Scout/Sniper team was inserted into the training area prior to the actual battalion exercise. Our team was brought in by a Chinook helicopter as it hovered its rear exit hatch on the edge of a mountain peak. The landing felt somewhat unstable as we waited for the ramp to go down so that we could get out and hike to our position. The pilot must have been damn good to have hovered the way he did; however, we did not want to be in there any longer than we had to. Once we exited with our gear on the mountain, we oriented ourselves and moved toward our tentative observation post which was about two to three miles away.

Once in our mountaintop position overlooking the desert valley, our team was tasked with calling in artillery on the "advancing enemy" as the training commenced. There were also trenches set up in the valley to depict enemy defenses. Sgt Joseph was calling in artillery on these positions, when he then told me that it was my turn. He handed me the binoculars as I conducted my measurements with the markers built into the optics.

I radioed my coordinates to the artillery unit with the team radio so that they could fire a single round with which I could adjust fire if necessary. Sgt Joseph then asked if I was sure about the coordinates I gave to the artillery unit and I told him yes. The first artillery round landed right near the trench, and I felt that it was a close enough hit. I then called in a fire for effect (or a barrage) on the enemy position. Multiple artillery rounds then landed just outside and inside of the trench. "I guess your coordinates were right after all," Sgt Joseph remarked.

## 7. Scout/Sniper Platoon

Sometime after the combined arms exercise at Camp Wilson, the time came when the 3rd Battalion 4th Marines Scout/Sniper platoon would run an indoc to increase the size of the unit. I would help run the indoc with Sgt Shane and Sgt Joseph. The Marines that tried out for the platoon would come from the companies within the battalion as they did before. The training conducted would be in a manner similar to what I experienced the year prior; however, with fewer people to supervise the exercises. Marines who would participate in the event would mainly come from India and Lima companies.

There were maybe twenty to thirty Marines who tried out for the platoon and by the end of the first day of the indoc, that group had shrunk by more than half. The majority of the Marines who quit I believe had done so during the sandbag run through the small mountain range on the Twenty-Nine Palms base. After about two weeks into receiving the new members of the platoon, only about ten Marines remained. It would be with this group of guys that I would form the strongest brotherhood during my time in the Marine Corps.

In late 2003, the battalion was slotted for deployment to Okinawa, Japan. This was a typical Marine Corps deployment and was not out of the ordinary. Prior to leaving for Japan, a Marine by the name of Cpl Dunham from "8th and I" was assigned to our battalion. He would eventually deploy back to Iraq with the 7th Marines. At this time, he was assigned to Kilo Company and assisted them with training other Marines until his eventual transfer out of the 3rd Battalion 4th Marines prior to the Okinawa deployment.

# Deployment II: Operation Iraqi Freedom II
*(January to July 2004)*

# 8

# Haditha

The bulk of the training in Okinawa took place on Camp Schwab in a classroom located close to the barracks on base. Our platoon would usually conduct physical training every morning, followed by classroom instruction, with some intermittent hazing thrown in for good measure. The classroom instruction mostly repeated everything provided by the Scout/Sniper School at Camp Pendleton. We continued to go over Scout/Sniper definitions verbatim and were constantly conducting observation exercises. If someone in the platoon fell asleep during a course of instruction in the classroom, the Marine would have to take a "drink" to help him wake up. This meant that the Marine would have to run out of the room and jump into the ocean about two hundred yards away.

After jumping into the sea, the Marine would then return to the classroom soaking wet as he sat at his desk "attentively." The definitions were the same as those I had memorized when I initially joined the platoon. The eight "R's" of observation were pressed into our memory by reciting each element while doing burpees. With each movement we would shout in unison, "Realize, Recognize, Record, Recall, Review, Recite, Respond, Reassess!"

While in Japan, the platoon was set to attend the Marine Corps Special Operations Training Group (SOTG) training course. The SOTG course was tailored to the Marine Corps Scout/Sniper platoons with an emphasis on patrolling techniques in the jungle along with M-40 sniper rifle marksmanship. Once arriving at the SOTG section, the platoon gathered in a classroom on Camp Hansen, Okinawa, where we met with one of the instructors. He was a Caucasian

## Deployment II: Operation Iraqi Freedom II

first sergeant and was somewhat stocky. As he introduced himself and proceeded with what the SOTG course included, I got the sense he was very confident, almost to the point of arrogance. However, he was a Marine SOTG instructor, so his personality came as no surprise.

The next portion of the SOTG course included the "Jungle Ambush" patrol. My platoon was organized into two-man teams and would conduct live fire on a timed course. The instructors looked for good patrolling techniques coupled with firearms accuracy. The course was linear as each team patrolled within the designated section and would engage targets as they presented themselves. I was paired up with a platoon member by the name of Dean for the ambush section. Dean was one of the newer guys who tried out during the second indoc; however, we got along well.

We conducted our patrol through the jungle as the instructors called out each particular target for engagement. Dean and I hit our targets as we continued up the designated route. We continued to move and shoot the targets until the course was completed. We were then told by the instructors that Dean and I completed the course with the best score.

One day while on Camp Schwab, the battalion gathered at the base theater for a briefing from the commander of the 1st Marine Division, General Mattis. We shuffled into the building as we awaited his arrival. Once General Mattis walked onto the stage, he greeted the Marines in attendance. We responded with a loud and thunderous, "Er rah!" We as Marines had a tremendous amount of respect for General Mattis because he was straightforward, and there was a feeling that he genuinely cared for his troops.

General Mattis went on to congratulate our battalion on a job well done during Operation Iraqi Freedom. He then proceeded to brief the battalion on the current situation in Iraq. I for one knew, as I am sure many others did, that the situation with the Army in Iraq was not going exactly according to plan. I had recently read the front of an article on the *Marine Corps Times* newspaper that the death toll in Iraq had reached 500 American war dead by early 2004. During a question-and-answer period with General Mattis, one Marine asked

## 8. Haditha

if the battalion was going back to Iraq. General Mattis stated that the battalion would absolutely not return to Iraq.

A few weeks later, the order came down to the battalion that we would return to the Middle East. The United States military stabilization plan in Iraq was not going too well and violence was still prevalent in the country. About two days prior to deploying back to Kuwait, Doc, and I, along with Dean, decided to go out for a night in the town for some last-minute fun. "Doc" as we called him was our Scout/Sniper platoon Corpsman. He was a tall, thin Caucasian male in his early twenties and was in phenomenal shape.

Our battalion had been restricted from leaving base in the days leading up to the deployment; however, we were determined to go out and have a good time anyway. It was about nine in the evening when we decided that we would leave camp by jumping the gate in the motor pool area that was adjacent to a main highway leading away from our base. We sneaked into the motor pool area under the cover of darkness and proceeded to jump the chain link fence which was also topped with razor wire. We somehow managed to jump the gate without sustaining any serious injury and walked toward the bar we usually had drinks at.

Once there, we were greeted by the employees and started having a few beers. We would drink and talk with the workers as they tried to convince us to buy them overpriced alcoholic beverages as expected. After about two hours of consistently drinking beers, we came up with the idea of getting more drinks further into town. Doc brought up the prospect of trying the infamous Habu Sake at one of the local bars; therefore, we managed to make our way to one of the more authentic Japanese establishments that were less inclined to cater to the typical Marine crowd.

Once we made our way into one of the bars, we spoke with the barkeep and asked for the Habu Sake. He then showed us the bottle that the drink came in which contained a snake head. At this point, we were all somewhat drunk and asked for shots of the exotic liquor. We took several swigs each and eventually managed to make our way back toward the bar we had started with near base. Luckily, we were able to hitch a ride from a new lieutenant from Kilo Company

## Deployment II: Operation Iraqi Freedom II

which took us back onto Camp Schwab. He had driven a van that happened to be at the same establishment where we were as he was picking up other Marines. He was there to safely get his men back onto base.

The lieutenant knew we had been drinking and managed to get us back to our barracks area without issue. Dean and I still wanted to keep the party going so we decided that we should go off base again to get more drinks. This decision was fueled by the alcohol that was already in our systems. Soon after, we were off camp and managed to make our way back to the nearby bar for more beers.

When the time came for the deployment back to the Middle East, the 3rd Battalion 4th Marines would again fly over to Kuwait and would eventually stage at Camp Victory. Once at base, the battalion would receive a briefing on the current situation in Iraq. There were slideshows describing the different ethnic groups, opposing forces, and tactics used by the enemy against the allied coalition. It appeared that Improvised Explosive Devices, also known as "IEDs," were used to great effect against the American military. The most commonly used IED was the roadside bomb, which was typically an artillery round placed on the side of the road and wired for detonation against American or allied military vehicles.

Many of the IEDs could be hidden inside trash, animal carcasses, or broken-down vehicles. Just as with any boobytrap utilized in a war, the possibilities of their concealment were limited only by the imagination of the people placing them. The insurgents knew that they stood very little chance against the American military in a head-on fight, so they resorted to ambush/boobytrap tactics, much in the way the Viet Cong did in the Vietnam War. The insurgents would also place a lot of pressure on the allied Iraqi military; again, just as the North Vietnamese and Vietcong had against the South Vietnamese military during the war in Southeast Asia that took place in the 1960s.

After receiving the briefings, our Scout/Sniper platoon would situate itself into one of the large tents at Camp Victory. This would be our temporary housing until we would be ordered to go back into Iraq for combat operations. The base had many amenities such as fast-food restaurants, a large exchange, places for haircuts, and little shops

## 8. Haditha

where one could buy Middle Eastern merchandise. As in any war, there was a little economy in and of itself at these coalition camps.

Prior to leaving for Kuwait, I was able to stay in contact with my then wife Stephanie and we realized that we would be stationed in the same area. Stephanie happened to be at Camp Victory during my brief stay there. She was located nearby with her unit, and we would meet up one afternoon. I would meet her at her company tent, where I met with other members of her unit. We then went to her bed within the tent that was sectioned off with sheets. We lay down on her cot and simply caught up on life. We were both very happy to see each other.

When evening came, we would make our way to her Army transport vehicle which she had operated in during her missions in Iraq. We ended up sleeping together in the rear passenger compartment of the vehicle and then simply lay there while talking some more. She knew I had to leave soon to Iraq and the thought of possibly not seeing each other again was in the back of my mind. We made the most of the little time we had together.

A few days would pass before the 3rd Battalion 4th Marines was ordered to leave Camp Victory. The unit would be tasked with replacing a United States Army Cavalry unit at the Haditha Dam in Iraq. The 75th Ranger Regiment had secured the dam the year prior during the 2003 invasion. The Army Cavalry unit likely had been there since the initial battle took place and were continuously conducting security operations in the area. They had taken some losses from skirmishes and IEDs.

The battalion would conduct a "left seat, right seat" with the cavalry unit to familiarize ourselves with the tempo of operations in that region. Our platoon would look for several different areas that we could conduct observation posts from in order to prevent insurgents placing roadside bombs on U.S. military routes. Once the battalion set in and became familiar with the Haditha area, our platoon had set up in a large room within the Haditha Dam. The rest of the unit would be set up in other rooms throughout the facility as well. The Azerbaijan military occupied the structure too. Their main focus was to provide security at posts throughout the dam, which freed up Marines to go out on patrol for security operations.

# Deployment II: Operation Iraqi Freedom II

One afternoon, Mason (who had joined the Scout/Sniper platoon from the second indoc) and Sgt Shane set out on a reconnaissance patrol with a contingent belonging to the Army Cavalry unit. After their patrol had been completed, Mason and Sgt Shane returned to the Haditha Dam forward operating base. Mason mentioned that during the patrol, an IED was set off near one of the cavalry armored vehicles. The Army unit then immediately fired into the nearby palm grove, believing that spotters might be hiding nearby. Mason seemed distraught over the incident, and it was his first IED experience in the Iraq War.

In about the second week of occupying the Haditha Dam, the base was attacked by several mortar rounds that did not kill or injure any coalition forces. However, the short bombardment shook up Dalton, another new member to the Scout/Sniper platoon, who was on his first Iraq deployment. It was almost amusing to see the reactions of the Marines who were not a part of the invasion and were now experiencing the sporadic attacks. It seemed that the typical reaction was fear and worry. That was understandable because they had never experienced any type of combat up to that point in their enlistments.

For my second deployment, I would be assigned to Sgt Shane's section with Mason and Dean. I felt that we had a good team, and we became close during our stay in Okinawa, Japan. Dean and I would eventually perform almost countless observation posts together overlooking random roads. To me, the deployment so far was absolutely boring and seemed to drag on. Having experienced the fast-paced battles of the invasion, this new form of "warfare" was monotonous.

During the initial weeks of the deployment, it seemed that the battalion Combined Anti Armor Team, or "CAAT" as they were referred to, were consistently being attacked with potshots and the occasional IEDs inside and around Haditha itself. I specifically recall hearing about a grenade incident where an insurgent attempted to throw a frag at one of the Humvees and then fled. There would be frequent raids on suspected High Value Target (HVT) locations in hopes of capturing/killing an insurgent leader or a former Saddam Hussein era higher ranking officer.

Conducting foot patrols in the area of Haditha was also a

## 8. Haditha

common occurrence. These types of missions would usually last only a few hours. Much of the aim during the foot patrols was to be highly visible; however, if enemy combatants or caches were discovered, that would be dealt with as well. I did not engage or confront any enemy combatants up to that point in my deployment.

The Haditha Dam had small islands located within the body of water that it held back for the nearby citizens of Iraq. Higher command felt that those islands had to be patrolled for any possible enemy insurgents—or they just wanted to consume the Marines' time to stave off boredom. Dean and I were attached to a squad from Kilo Company that would go with the Marine Zodiac attachment who operated the small black rubber boats typically used for Reconnaissance insertions. The insertion would take place during the early afternoon with a squad assigned to about three Zodiacs.

Our team would land on a small island about half a mile away from the Haditha Dam. We patrolled the small patch of land with the Kilo Company squad and, as expected, met no resistance. I would not go into any mission with the idea that something might not happen; however, it was unlikely that a group of insurgents would take the time to land on the island and perform any type of attack from there. I think the mission was given to us as more of a training exercise.

The Scout/Sniper platoon that I was a part of did have a satellite phone which probably would have been the equivalent of gold in some Marines' eyes back in the United States. The "sat" phone was our link back home that we could use to reach out to our friends and family with. The wireless satellite phone at that time in Iraq was a rare commodity and each member of the section would take turns using it.

Much of my stay at the Haditha Dam was taken up with observation post after observation post on the side of some mundane road, which appeared at times to be in the middle of nowhere. However, the roads our Scout/Sniper teams would watch were continuous targets for IEDs placed by the Iraqi insurgency. The missions would typically last about two to three days, with only a two-man team. The shifts rotated by each man would last anywhere from two to six hours, while the other team member rested.

During the posts, it seemed that there was nothing but time to sit

## Deployment II: Operation Iraqi Freedom II

there on the optics and reflect on your life. That is simply how much time there was to think while hiding on a hill near the side of a long Iraqi road on the outskirts of Haditha. I can say I probably recalled almost every single life event while performing these types of missions. Given the time spent during these posts, you would also learn a lot about the person you were paired up with.

The rather boring task of watching roads would soon be interrupted by violence that I had never experienced up to that time. On March 31, 2004, news would come out that a team of American Blackwater contractors had been ambushed while passing through the city of Fallujah, Iraq. The attack was conducted by Iraqi insurgents who then pulled the American bodies out of their vehicle and burned them. The Americans were then hung over a bridge on the Euphrates River *(https://en.wikipedia.org/wiki/2004_Fallujah_ambush)*. The Fallujah ambush would cause anger within the United States and the American military.

In response to the American contractors' deaths, units within the United States Marine Corps and Army in Iraq would be tasked with clearing out the insurgent stronghold of Fallujah. My unit, the 3rd Battalion 4th Marines, would be moved from our base in Haditha, and would eventually make our way toward Camp Al-Asad in March of 2004 for the upcoming Fallujah operation. The movement to Al-Asad would be uneventful in that there were no attacks on the convoy toward the base. The battalion arrived at Camp Al-Asad in the late evening and the 7-ton transport trucks that most of the Marines rode in parked in an open lot on the large base. We then dismounted the vehicles and looked for a place on the dirt ground to sleep on for the night. I used my pack as a pillow as I had done many times before while utilizing my poncho liner for a blanket. I eventually fell asleep after getting situated in preparation for the following day.

# 9

# The Battle for Fallujah

"Incoming!" shouted a nearby Staff Sgt from Kilo Company. I woke up panicked from a deep sleep and was frantically looking for a place to hide from the incoming munitions. "Get your fucking helmets and vests on!" he continued yelling at the top of his lungs. I could hear the loud screeching of incoming rockets followed by large concussive explosions. The rockets probably landed about 25 to 50 yards away from our positions in rapid succession of about five to eight rounds.

It was terrifying to say the least. It felt like I could not get my helmet and flak vest on fast enough as everyone scrambled to get their gear on. It was a horrible feeling knowing that at any second a rocket could land on or near you and nothing could be done about it except try to get cover. The ordeal was over just about as fast as it started but had been terrifying. The thought of rockets screeching in from overhead with no place to hide made me feel vulnerable. The rockets could land anywhere and all I could do was hope that one did not land on me and blow me to pieces.

After the rocket attack, we accounted for each other and eventually went back to sleep. The following morning, the battalion would move out in a large convoy to Camp Fallujah. The movement to the forward operating base would be uneventful, as there were no ambushes or IEDs encountered along the way. Once the battalion arrived at Camp Fallujah, there it would become part of the Regimental Combat Team 1. This multi-battalion task force would take part in what was to become known as Operation Vigilant Resolve, also known as the "First Battle of Fallujah." Once the battalion was set in its respective

## Deployment II: Operation Iraqi Freedom II

area, we were able to move about the camp to utilize the Marine Corps Exchange as well as other amenities offered there. I eventually made my way to the base's phone center near the MCX.

Military/civilian members who were on the camp could use the phones at this center to call their friends and family back home. The complex was in a small, fabricated building similar to those used at construction sites and each phone booth was separated by a small wall. Utilizing my phone card, I called my older sister back home in California. When I reached her, she asked me how I was doing. I told her that I was fine, and I was stationed somewhere near Fallujah, Iraq. I then told her about what happened the night before.

I told her about the rocket attack in some degree of detail while attempting to convey a positive attitude about what occurred that night prior. Her end of the phone suddenly fell silent for a few seconds followed up by my sister sobbing while trying to talk. I apologized for telling her about the incident. She then said that she just wanted me to come back home safe and I told her that I would be ok. It was a very emotional phone call. She told me she loved me and to be safe as we ended the conversation.

At Camp Fallujah, the scene was quite chaotic. The artillery from the base was continuously being fired off onto enemy positions and special operations/conventional forces were seen everywhere. The following morning during breakfast, our meal was suddenly interrupted by loud explosions. Initially people in the chow hall tent were anxious as to what the noise was; then it became apparent that the base artillery battery had just fired off rounds.

Preparations for the upcoming operation would take place at Camp Fallujah and briefings for the upcoming assault were continuous. As a team leader with the Scout/Sniper platoon, I met with the lieutenant from 1st platoon, Kilo Company in his area tent. He was a young second lieutenant, somewhat baby faced, but rather stocky. Dean and I introduced ourselves at which time we requested a two-man security team from his platoon to assist us when the assault began.

After speaking with the lieutenant, Dean and I hung out with some of the guys from Kilo Company 1st platoon. It was about

## 9. The Battle for Fallujah

8:00 p.m. and almost everyone in the tent was standing while going over orders. Some were joking around. There was a mood of excitement mixed with a little bit of anxiety when a sudden a burst of automatic weapons fire was heard from the compound wall, about fifty yards away. The crack of the rounds zipped by the tent and everyone, almost all at once, dropped to the floor onto their stomachs. It seemed as if everyone panicked at the same time.

It was not an uncontrollable panic, but a panic nonetheless because no one knew exactly where the gunfire was coming from. There was no doubt in my mind that it was not friendlies firing and the burst of gunfire had been directed at the tents. All members at the company area grabbed their rifles and ran outside to meet the attackers. There was no second guessing by anyone to meet the threat, the reaction was almost automatic. My adrenaline was pumping frantically. What kind of attack was this? How many were there?

As we ran out of the tent, the Company Commander from Kilo Company ran his leg across a tent stake to which a rope was tied. The hinge tore into his left calf. The injury was not too serious; however, it was enough to cause him to limp to the defensive line where Marines had set up near the compound wall. As I ran to the line, I heard Sgt Shane yell out to me, "Brian, come this way!" He was setting up the M-40 on the rear of the 7-ton truck.

I met him at the truck as we both set up our rifles on the roof of the troop carrier. Our line of sight was above the defensive position below. Marines were yelling and shooting at the area where they believed the insurgents were jumping over. It was very dark as the camp was void of artificial light for security purposes. After a brief standoff of about five minutes, the order to cease fire was given. I did not fire a single round.

I had not seen who or exactly where the attackers were. I later heard that it was a three to five-man team that sprayed their AK-47s over the compound wall and were shot as they attempted to jump over the barrier. I was surprised that the enemy was bold enough to try and breach the compound wall in that manner. Maybe the insurgents who attacked somehow knew Fallujah was going to be assaulted the next day and that was their own small way of trying to interrupt the plans.

## Deployment II: Operation Iraqi Freedom II

Or, it may just have been a random attack. This event would be a small taste of what was to come in the upcoming weeks.

The following morning, the battalion gathered in an open lot on the base for final preparations before the assault into the city. Last-minute briefings were given, and all equipment had been checked. Dean and I spoke to Kilo Company 1st platoon's lieutenant again about our supporting role with his unit. "When we get into the city, I want you guys to waste anyone with a rifle. I want you to shoot them so fast that they have no idea where it is coming from," said the lieutenant. It was strange to think that I was getting ready to partake in a large urban battle. There had been a year and half of MOUT training leading up to that day; however, I did not really know what to expect in a prolonged battle in that type of environment.

As we waited in the open lot on that clear, sunny day, the calm of the afternoon was interrupted by the command to load up into the AAVs and Humvees for the attack. Everyone loaded onto their respective vehicles. As we began exiting the camp, music came on over loudspeakers which were attached to certain AAVs. Disturbed's "Down with the Sickness" began blaring across the convoy in what seemed like an effort to pump us up. As the opening riff of the song played, Dean and I were sitting in the back of the Humvee attached to Kilo Company.

I had some anxiety about the operation; however, it was not overwhelming. It was a mix of anxiety and adrenaline. What would happen as we entered the city? How tough would the resistance be? The mission was to clear the city of insurgents, house by house. This was a daunting task to say the least, and just how daunting would later be felt when entering the insurgent stronghold of Fallujah.

We drove several miles from FOB Fallujah along a commonly traveled MSR leading up to the city. As we made our way along the road, U.S. artillery rounds from Camp Fallujah began screeching in from overhead and landing into the eastern portion of the city, in the vicinity of where Kilo Company was to assault. The noise of the incoming artillery rounds was abruptly accompanied by the loud concussive boom of their impacts. The fire support was intricately timed to cover our approach along the MSR and would end just prior to us

## 9. The Battle for Fallujah

getting into position for the push into the city. Once in position along the road just outside of Fallujah, Marines dismounted from their AAVs and formed a large skirmish line along the MSR. Dean and I dismounted from our Humvee as well. Marines were strung along the road and were either taking a knee or lying in the prone position with their weapons fixed on the city.

The AAVs then conducted a 90 degree turn from facing north on the road to facing directly west toward the town. The Humvees did the same. After about a five-minute wait, the order was given to push inward. Marines and armored vehicles, intermittently positioned, pushed alongside into the city in one long continuous line that seemed to stretch out for about a mile in both directions. It was a surreal feeling to participate in such a large-scale urban battle that had not taken place since 1968, in the city of Hue during the Vietnam War.

Marines and mechanized vehicles continued online while pushing into the city from east to west. As Marines spread among the buildings, groups then splintered off into different directions to clear structures. Within about the first block of entering the city, gunfire erupted on both sides. I could not tell exactly where the fire was coming from, but it was heard without a doubt. Dean and I then ran into a nearby building centered on the assault formation that overlooked a main street going from east to west. As we entered the building with our security element, we noticed that the complex was empty.

We set up a hide position overlooking the main street and during that time, all I could hear was gunfire coupled with Marines hollering. After positioning my M-40 rifle, I looked down my telescopic sight while focusing down the street. I noticed an Iraqi man, maybe in his forties, walking out of a building, perhaps his home, and simply standing there. Marines were yelling at him to come toward our position and surrender. Was he a lookout? Was he possibly armed? No one could have known for sure. He was maybe one-hundred yards from our main line as he then began walking away and toward the west side of his house.

Marines then fired in his direction as the rounds impacted all around him. He was not struck by the gunfire and simply continued walking westward toward the side of his home. I was amazed at how

# Deployment II: Operation Iraqi Freedom II

**Sitting in my hide position on the first day of the Battle for Fallujah (April 2004).**

calmly this man walked while bullets were striking the walls of the building around him. Some rounds came very close to his head. This was the second time I had seen something like this in Iraq and I was shocked that he survived. All this was observed through my scope, so I had an up close view of what that man was experiencing, yet I could do was simply watch with a sick feeling in my stomach that he would die from the gunfire. I was ready to fight for my fellow Marines, but I never got used to seeing people die in front of me.

The assault line on the first block of Fallujah held for maybe an hour until the formation began pushing further into the city. Dean and I exited the building that overlooked the street and were met with an AAV on the roadway. We spoke with the team leader from his hatch just outside the building we exited. We immediately noticed a moderate sized hole on the right side of the AAV's armor plating. I asked the team leader what happened, and he mentioned that an RPG was fired at them by an insurgent when they entered the city.

## 9. The Battle for Fallujah

With the amount of gunfire heard and the armored vehicle being struck so soon in the battle, my gut feeling told me we were in for a fight. We told each other to stay safe and then simply pushed inward about another block. At this point the fight intensified. The Kilo Company command post was set up around the left flank of the battalion assault force.

Dean and I made our way toward the command post, where we took up a position in a rather large abandoned home near Kilo Company. This building was butted against an MSR south of the company position. Again, the defensive lines were strung out from north to south, with armored vehicles and tanks positioned intermittently to support the infantry in the city.

Dean and I then left our position as we moved along the roof tops with our security team. We were checking the area along Kilo Company's southern flank for a better observation post. Our position was exposed as ricochets and rounds whizzed by overhead. For some reason we did not care, and we continued to walk along the rooftops while looking for a better hide position. We eventually made our way off the building and searched the nearby structures for a firing location. We cleared several Fallujah homes in our search as the battle was picking up pace at Kilo Company's command post.

Dean and I then eventually made our way to the Kilo Company command post. We entered the building and rushed toward the rooftop. Just as we exited the door that led to the rooftop, Marines nearby told us to watch out for incoming small arms fire. There was an enemy sniper shooting through the upper-level window which was adjacent to the door that we just used. I saw small holes in the metal door as we ran past where the sniper had been shooting. The insurgent was taking shots at the Marines as they ran past the door just before we got there. Dean and I immediately ran out of the kill zone while seeking cover nearby.

We immediately climbed onto a small perch that rose from the rooftop by maybe another six feet. This was not the best position tactically; however, the Marines were taking heavy fire and we had the best optics in that particular area that would be able to spot the shooter. I could hear Marines shouting from the lower ledge of the building

## Deployment II: Operation Iraqi Freedom II

that they were taking fire from an insurgent sniper and asked for our support.

I looked downward to where a Marine was furiously firing his light machine gun. As he fired, he looked up toward me then pointed westward at a building maybe two hundred yards away, saying that was where the sniper was shooting from. Dean and I were frantically looking through our optics for the enemy combatant. Dean was looking through the spotting scope as I looked through the sniper scope. My observation and train of thought was suddenly interrupted by the light machine gunner shouting, "Hey! Rounds are impacting just below you!" I then looked over the wall and saw a hole where a round impacted about four feet below my position.

I shrugged it off and dismissed the sniper as a bad shot. I then continued to frantically look through my scope for the insurgent position. I knew that other Marines were depending on us to find the sniper who continuously posed a threat. I also felt that I had decent cover behind the ledge on the rooftop. As I began looking for the shooter shortly after discovering the first bullet impact, I suddenly felt a violent burst of concrete bits fly onto my face. The insurgent sniper had shot a round toward my head, but the bullet struck the concrete ledge in front of my face instead.

Immediately after feeling the burst of concrete, I put my head and body as flat as possible against the roof top. A barrage of sniper rounds continued to crack over me. I was pinned down and that sniper wanted me dead. I was frightened by the initial impact that had almost ripped into my face as the other rounds continued to fly over my body, missing by mere inches. My ears rang with each sniper bullet cracking the air overhead.

The realization of just how close I had come to dying had set in again and my one thought was to just get off the roof as quickly as possible. As the barrage of sniper rounds continued to crack off inches from my head, I yelled at Dean to roll off the roof. We then threw ourselves off our position and fell onto the adjoining rooftop below. I was absolutely relieved to be off the ledge. I sat there thinking how close I came to death and how horrible that felt.

The fighting raged all around our position as Marines on our

## 9. The Battle for Fallujah

**Enemy sniper round impacts on my rooftop overwatch position. The impact on the top ledge missed my face by approximately three inches (April 2004).**

Northern flank were battling an insurgent stronghold just northwest of the command post. Dean and I got into a new position near a Forward Air Control (FAC) officer with his radio men. I began firing into the windows at the building down the street where I suspected the enemy sniper had recently shot from. Meanwhile Dean called to the AAV team nearby to fire grenade and .50 caliber machine gun rounds into the suspected sniper position.

The FAC officer appeared to be stressed about the continuous combat he was experiencing so far. He asked one of his radio operators to request something over the air. I don't think the radio operator heard the FAC officer due to the noise of the battle taking place. The

## Deployment II: Operation Iraqi Freedom II

FAC officer then repeated his request to his radio operator and yelled, "I'm not dying on this fucking rooftop in this shitty city! So, do what the fuck I ask!." He then asked the other radio operator to launch a smoke round at a suspected enemy position down the street.

His round found its mark in a nearby building and the officer excitedly told him about a job well done. After the smoke round was launched, the FAC officer contacted a Cobra attack helicopter over the radio and had it fire into the marked position. About a minute had passed when the sound of helicopter blades could be heard to our rear. The FAC officer was in continuous contact with the pilot via his radio and advised him of the marked target ahead of our lines.

The Cobra hovered low behind our building and then elevated itself into a firing position just over our heads. The gunship then fired two to three rockets into the marked position as the Marines in our building took cover behind a wall. Once the rockets collided into the

**View from my observation post during Operation Vigilant Resolve (April 2004).**

## 9. The Battle for Fallujah

suspected insurgent building, the FAC officer shouted with excitement. "That's what I'm talking about! That's how it's supposed to get done!"

During the frantic pace of the battle, we could hear someone speaking in Arabic on the loudspeakers positioned throughout the city. These loudspeakers are typically used for Muslim prayer throughout the day; however, we believed they were possibly being used to inform the insurgent fighters of our positions. I began shooting at the only loudspeakers that I could see with my M-40 rifle to disable them. At this time, an Iraqi man stood on a rooftop maybe one hundred yards to the west. He appeared unarmed and was looking toward our lines. I told Kilo Company, 1st platoon's leader, Lt Edmund about what I had just seen, and he replied, "Brian, you don't need to ask for my permission to shoot!"

From what I could see, the man was unarmed and may have been scouting our positions for the insurgents. I hesitantly placed my crosshairs over his head; however, I knew I would not feel right about shooting him at that time. It appeared to me that he was looking around to make sense of what was happening in his city. Yet, another part of me knew that we gave the Iraqi inhabitants plenty of warning to leave their town and this man was of military fighting age. As I contemplated taking his life, the man then went downstairs into the home.

The battle continued on as a squad from 1st platoon made entry into a house about half a block northwest of the command post. Shortly after their entry, we heard yelling coming from their area. We had gotten word over the radio that the squad encountered an enemy fighter in one of the rooms of the house. Explosions were heard as Marines were likely throwing grenades to clear out the enemy combatant.

Marines from 1st platoon then threw a canister of CS gas into the room where they had encountered the insurgent fighter. Shortly after, the CS gas floated upward toward our positions at the command post as I and other Marines on the rooftop began coughing violently. I rushed to get to my pack so that I could retrieve my gas mask. As I kneeled over my pack and frantically went through it, I continued coughing while oozing mucus from my nose. My eyes watered up from

## Deployment II: Operation Iraqi Freedom II

the chemical in the air as I hurriedly removed the gas mask from my pack and placed it over my face in hopes of getting relief. Once the mask was on, I began thinking of the craziness I found myself in.

A few minutes had passed when we heard more gunfire from the house. Marines from 1st platoon then pulled out an injured Marine from the building they were fighting in. The 1st squad leader, Cpl Danielson, had been shot by the insurgent in the home. Marines were frantically yelling for a medic and an evac as he was rushed away from the house on a stretcher.

Once Cpl Danielson was rushed away from the area, several Marines approached the outside of the insurgent stronghold, and one threw a satchel charge into the structure. The Marines then ran back

**AK assault rifles collected by my partner and me during our search of nearby homes during the First Battle of Fallujah. The collected rifles and ammunition were set up in our hide position.**

## 9. The Battle for Fallujah

toward 1st platoon's position as the satchel charge was set to explode with hopes of clearing out the enemy combatant. About thirty seconds after the satchel charge was thrown, a massive explosion was heard and felt. I thought that nothing could have possibly survived that with such a munition. Debris flew in about every direction and I was hit in the shin by a fist-sized piece of concrete. "Fuck!" I yelled as the chunk hit my leg. I was thinking what in the hell else can happen? I almost had my head blown off, my face felt like it had been on fire from the CS gas, Cpl Danielson had just been shot, and now a damn piece of brick just rammed into my shin!

Shortly after the satchel charge was utilized, 1st platoon was still taking fire from the ruins of the insurgent building. It was believed that the enemy combatants had that particular building tunneled and connected to the adjacent homes for quick movement. The Abrams tank attached to the assault force was then called up with hopes of finishing the job of destroying the stronghold. The tank fired off its main cannon into the rubble approximately three times over a rather short period of time.

# 10

# Halting the Advance

The battalion's Headquarters and Service (H & S) Company Commander was on the rooftop with us that day. As it became more and more apparent that this would not be a pushover fight, the H & S Company Commander stated, "Hey guys, they are going to try and hug tight onto our positions much like the Vietnamese did in Vietnam. They want to get as close as possible so that we do not want to use our air and artillery support." The thought of having to clear out every building in the city of Fallujah seemed to be a more daunting task after experiencing the first day of the battle.

I then began to think about how the soldiers from World War II must have felt fighting in the European cities on their way toward Germany. Or how the Marines must have felt fighting their way through the city of Hue during the Vietnam War. I was simply getting a taste of the hardships they must have experienced in those urban combat situations. How long will it take us to clear Fallujah? How many Marines will be injured or killed on our way to the center of the town? These thoughts quickly ran through my mind as the battle went on.

It was getting closer to evening as the battle still raged on. Dean was on shift while on the rooftop as I headed downstairs to the second story of the occupied Iraqi home. A few other Marines on the second story were taking a break from the battle as well. I joined them and lay down on the hard concrete floor while utilizing my pack as a pillow. I rested there thinking how close I had come to dying in my encounter with the enemy sniper. How close those rounds came to my head and how the sniper was determined to kill me.

As I lay there, I could hear the loud concussive noise of machine

## 10. Halting the Advance

guns, explosions, and Marines yelling. The frantic pace of the battle did not seem to slow down. I heard one of Kilo Company's staff sergeants interrogating a captured Iraqi male on the first floor of the building. "Are you Mujahedeen? Huh, motherfucker?!" I could hear the staff sergeant yell through the noise of machine gun fire and explosions going off nearby. He suspected the Iraqi man of being an insurgent. "No! No Mujahedeen!" the Iraqi man replied. "Fucking bullshit!" the Staff Sergeant immediately shouted back. The chaos of the battle just continued on. This was an urban battle where the enemy could be anywhere and everywhere with almost limitless places to hide. The enemy combatants could fire from windows, behind walls, rooftops, or even from the sewers if they chose to.

Later in the evening, I positioned myself back onto the rooftop as I scanned the area with my night vision goggles. Firing and explosions could still be heard throughout the city. I continued to scan the area for any enemy movement. Suddenly, I heard the sound of incoming artillery rounds. The artillery rounds landed about a hundred yards to the south of our position in rapid succession. About five artillery rounds landed in a linear pattern along the street in what appeared to be a protective bombardment.

The following morning was rather quiet, up until the Muslim prayer could be heard over the other loudspeakers positioned throughout the city. Hearing the prayer reminded me of just how far from home I really was and just how foreign a land we found ourselves in. Our sector remained calm with the exception of the random potshots from the insurgents and intermittent enemy mortar rounds. Afternoon came in with the sound of prayer yet again echoing throughout the area.

As Dean and I were on the rooftop of Kilo Company's command post, we were scouting the surrounding buildings with our optics when we heard what sounded like a man yelling for help. I then heard a woman and small girl yelling for help as well. I looked over the rooftop ledge to see where the voices were coming from. I looked over to the west and saw a family reaching out of a metal barred window for help from a nearby home.

This family yelling was maybe fifty yards ahead of our lines and

## Deployment II: Operation Iraqi Freedom II

the building that they were in was on fire. Smoke was billowing out of the window they reached out from. The family's cry for help intensified and I thought they were going to be burned alive. My heart sank as I waited for the screams. About four Marines who were already at floor level rushed across the street to the family who were desperately yelling out.

The family continued to plead for help as the fire increased in intensity. Once the group of Marines reached the building, one of them frantically pulled at the bars covering the window. After about a minute, the Marine was able to pull one of the bars free which was just enough room to start bringing out the family from the window, one by one. Everyone was pulled out of the burning building safely and I was relieved.

The following morning, Sgt Shane requested that Dean and I accompany him at his position approximately a hundred yards north of Kilo Company's command post. When we arrived, the first thing I noticed was the horrible smell. It was the aroma of rotting flesh wafting throughout the warm air. Looking onto the street from their observation position, I could see enemy bodies strewn across and down the MSR that was being watched by Sgt Shane as well as Marines from Kilo Company, 2nd platoon. Later that day, while I was conducting overwatch with Dean, two Iraqi men walked up on our position. Neither was armed and Mason, who had been with Sgt Shane at the start of the battle, told the men to leave the area. Both of the Iraqis then left. Dalton, a newer member of the platoon, also accompanied Sgt Shane's team that day.

Sgt Shane had been asleep at the time the Iraqi men stumbled upon our position. When he heard of this, he became upset and asked Mason why he had not shot them. Mason mentioned that the men were unarmed. "I don't give a fuck!" Sgt Shane replied. "They were probably scouting our position! Next time someone comes up on our position you shoot the assholes!" Sgt Shane was obviously worried that the Iraqi men would report our observation post to other insurgent fighters.

Just down the main road that our observation post overlooked there were several previously shot-up Iraqi cars. In one particular

## 10. Halting the Advance

vehicle, someone could be seen moving through the rear of the passenger compartment. I trained my sights on the movement in the vehicle. It appeared that someone was hiding in the back seat and not leaving the car.

Not chancing other Marines' being ambushed should they pass the vehicle, I shot at the passenger through the trunk of the car with the SASR (Special Application Scoped Rifle). This rifle was typically used to shoot through barriers such as cinder block walls or through light armored vehicles. The round that the SASR expended was .50 caliber. I shot one more time to ensure that the round passed through the rear of the car. The movement in the back seat then stopped. My hands were shaking as my heart raced from having killed someone through such close sight. One minute this person was moving, the next they were not.

Later that afternoon, Sgt Shane made it clear that he wanted to obtain a new position overlooking Kilo Company's northern flank. Our team ran across the street from our previously occupied building toward a position west of 2nd platoon's location. We made our way into the courtyard of the large concrete home. We then saw an older Iraqi man and a child standing there. The older man smiled and was apparently greeting us. The child was just standing there. The kid looked distraught and confused as I could see drag marks with blood on the ground which led to the rear of the home.

The First Battle of Fallujah was raging all around the child and I'm sure it would have been difficult for any six to seven-year-old to process what was happening. I then checked the back side of the home and was taken aback by the sight of a grave mound four feet in front of where I stood. They had buried one of their recently deceased family members who had been killed during the battle. We searched the outer area of the home for other members of the house or possible enemy fighters.

Mason stayed with the older man and child while the rest of our team cleared the inside of the large house. During our search, Dean found an AK rifle in the closet of the master bedroom. No one was found in the building. We then met with Mason downstairs in the courtyard. We advised 2nd platoon that we would be sending out

## Deployment II: Operation Iraqi Freedom II

the Iraqi man and child toward their lines. We needed them out of our area so that we could set up overwatch positions along the MSR. Both the man and child were sent away from the courtyard without incident.

The team would settle into the newly acquired position as we set up two observation posts within the large home. It was my turn for watch when I was woken up by Dean. I sat in the OP that overlooked the southern area of our position within the second story. About ten minutes had passed when I saw an enemy scout running eastward about one block south of our post. He had run past a building from down the street which allowed him to pass into my view through an open lot. I immediately got behind my M-40 sniper scope and followed him as he continued to run westward on the street, about eighty yards from my position. I slightly led him with my optic at about chest height until I fired off a single round.

The shot rang out as the insurgent immediately fell onto the street. He sat there yelling and moaning as I yelled up to Sgt Shane about the enemy scout. I then shot him in the chest with another round from the M-40. He continued yelling. "He's not going down!" I yelled up to Sgt Shane. I could not believe it. How could this man survive two 7.62mm rounds to the chest area?

"Fucking shoot him again!" I heard Sgt Shane yell from the rooftop. There was no way any Marine or Corpsman would run to the scout's aid without taking enemy fire at the distance he fell at. I then trained my rifle on his head and fired one more round to put him out of his misery. His yelling immediately stopped. It was a surreal experience having seen someone you shot so close-up through a scope, so clearly. It was a very personal and brutal thing to see. My body was shaking from nerves.

After the scout incident, Dalton sat with me at our post. It was his turn to observe with the optics as I lay down to take a nap. I was in a deep sleep when I was suddenly and violently awakened by several loud M40 rifle shots from inside the room. I was so startled from my nap that it felt like my heart was about to burst out of my chest. My adrenaline soared as I quickly got up to my feet. I looked over at Dalton as he finished his last shot. "Holy fuck! There were three of them

## 10. Halting the Advance

with AK's walking down the street! I got two of them and the other one ran off!"

Dalton was frantically looking through the scope of the rifle for other fighters. Apparently, he shot one of the insurgents who was walking down the road. One then ran off as the third fighter ran behind a berm, believing the shots came from the south, when Dalton was in fact firing from a northern position. This placed the fighter's back exposed to Dalton and that is when he was shot dead as well.

Throughout the day, when we needed to relieve ourselves, we would urinate on the side of the house. Every time I would pee there, I had to look at the mound of dirt where the child's family member was laid to rest. The mound was about four feet from where we used the bathroom and was eerie to see. It was a weird feeling of having a battle take place around me as I went to the bathroom next to someone's gravesite at their own home.

As the day transitioned into night, it was my turn at the observation position in the downstairs bedroom yet again. Dalton and Sgt Shane were on the rooftop post. I was looking through the night vision scope across the street where Dalton had recently killed the two enemy fighters, whose bodies still lay where they had been shot. As I continued to scan the nearby area and windows, I suddenly heard sporadic gunfire from 2nd platoon's position to our east. "Contact!" I heard some of the Marines from 2nd platoon yelling.

The sporadic gunfire turned into a loud continuous roar which lit up the entire previously pitch-black street. It looked as if it suddenly became daytime due to the muzzle flashes from the platoon's arsenal. The mixture of M-16s, M-249s, and AKs were booming off as 2nd platoon was fighting off a nearby enemy attack. I also heard shooting from the upstairs rooftop position. Dalton and Sgt Shane had joined in on the fight.

As the shooting raged on, I continued to scan the nearby area across the street from my post. I was almost certain that enemy fighters would try to attack our position from there. There was a nearby wall across the street that would have given the attackers plenty of cover leading up to our building. I trained the scope on the edge of the aforementioned wall, waiting for the fighters to rush toward us.

## Deployment II: Operation Iraqi Freedom II

The attack on our position never came. After a few minutes, the firefight from 2nd platoon's area ended and I could hear Marines yelling, "Cease fire!"

I asked Dalton how the firefight started. He mentioned that a squad of enemy fighters was seen running into a nearby building to the south across the street from 2nd platoon, which then started firing on the enemy position while the insurgents shot back. During the exchange, AK rounds and RPGs had been seen fired from the enemy position toward 2nd platoon. The violence of the exchange could not be overstated. The clash of the battle had been deafening and was quite scary. I would be the first to admit that I felt some fear; however, not enough to prevent me from performing my job during the firefight.

The following morning, I heard Sgt Shane fire from his position on the rooftop of the building we occupied. He mentioned that an insurgent sniper had been crawling up a tree approximately four hundred yards away to our west. It was a relief to hear because we had been taking potshots as we moved around the rooftop since we had been there.

That night during the battle, our team sat on the rooftop hide position as we all put some dip in our mouths and tried to relax. It was about nine in the evening and explosions could still be heard throughout the city. AC-130 gunships were firing on nearby enemy positions in the area. Although you could not see the gunships, they were continuously overhead providing protection for the ground troops participating in the battle. I grabbed a pair of night vision goggles and looked toward the partially cloud covered sky. Through the goggles I could see multiple infrared spotlights beaming downward from the sky and onto the ground in Fallujah. There were multiple spotlights, all focused on different areas of the battlefield.

Unless the insurgents had night vision goggles, they were unable to see the AC-130 spotlights. There were about five different infrared beams pointed at different positions in the city. Marine Psy Ops helicopters could also be heard playing AC/DC music in hopes of provoking the insurgents to fight so that they would expose their positions. The music was probably provided as a morale boost to the Marine ground forces as well.

## 10. Halting the Advance

One day during the battle, while still in our observation post, it was my turn for overwatch that afternoon. I sat down on the table in our dark room with my rifle set up on the table about four feet away from the window, facing west. We had been taking sporadic AK and sniper fire from that portion of the city continuously. From the west, approximately four hundred yards down the road where it split off into a T-intersection, I saw a male poke his head around a wall from the south corner. He was looking down the MSR and eastward toward the Marines' positions with binoculars.

He would go back behind the corner and then reappear while looking toward our positions. He looked like he might have been in his late teens. From his actions, he was likely a spotter for the insurgent fighters and was reporting what he saw to whoever was behind the wall, possibly a mortar team. I yelled up to Sgt Shane what I was seeing. He then replied, "Well, shoot his ass."

As the Iraqi male reappeared, he squatted behind the nearby bush, facing our lines with his binoculars yet again. I then placed my crosshairs over his chest, just below his neck. I had my sights trained on him for approximately five seconds before I pulled the trigger. After the shot, the Iraqi observer immediately dropped behind the bush from where he had been crouching. My heart was racing. I felt I had done the right thing in preventing the fighters from receiving intelligence on our positions; however, knowing I likely killed a teen weighed heavy on my conscience.

It was a war and a nasty battle. In my mind, there was no choice of sparing that teen's life at the expense of my life or my fellow Marines. I continued to look through my scope while searching the area for other fighters or observers. About five minutes into the search, an Iraqi ambulance pulled up behind the shrub where the Iraqi teen had just been seen. The ambulance crew then exited their vehicle and tended to the body.

During our time in the Iraqi home we occupied during the battle, dead insurgents were strewn about the street around our post. There was one deceased Iraqi male near our post, which we could constantly smell. "Brian, I need you to burn that body in the street," Sgt Shane told me due to the horrible odor emitting from the dead insurgent. Sgt

## Deployment II: Operation Iraqi Freedom II

Shane then doused a white sheet with gasoline, which he had found in the house.

He then gave me the sheet with a lighter. "Go put this over the body as quickly as possible and light it on fire." I wasn't too comfortable with the idea of running out onto the street during daytime, in a combat zone where insurgents had been taking shots at us daily. I expressed my concern to Sgt Shane regarding insurgent snipers. "Dean and I will cover you." I grabbed the gas covered sheet and lighter. I then approached the side gate of our occupied building. I did a quick prayer and immediately ran off toward the body which was about forty feet in front of our hide position.

The body lay in the gutter on the street. I then immediately covered the body and tried to light the sheet on fire. The damn lighter would not catch the spark. I was frantic as I continued to flick away at the lighter hoping to ignite the sheet. The thought of an enemy sniper shooting at me raced through my mind. After about eight attempts, the sheet caught fire and I sprinted back toward the side gate for cover. I then locked the gate and ran back upstairs to our hide position.

During the lull in the battle, a Red Crescent ambulance van drove toward our position from the east/west MSR adjacent to our building. The ambulance van parked nearby on the street where several of the dead bodies lay. An Iraqi man exited the vehicle and shouted, "Hello? Helllooo?" He was there to recover the corpses on the ground. The Red Crescent is the Middle Eastern equivalent of the Red Cross; therefore, he could recover the bodies and was considered a neutral party. Crew members from the ambulance quickly recovered the bodies and left shortly thereafter.

Later that evening, our team reflected on the Red Crescent ambulance driver, and we somewhat laughed at the situation. Here was this crew member, walking around the middle of the street in a combat zone, and he could not see anyone else nearby while bodies were strewn about. He was walking around and simply saying, "Hello?" while trying to reach out to someone. He probably felt like the loneliest man in the world at that time.

The following day, Dean and I decided to search the nearby buildings just outside of the company lines. We grabbed our flak vests and

## 10. Halting the Advance

pistols so that it would be easier for us to maneuver during our search of the houses. We then jumped the nearby wall just west of our position. We slowly searched the first house past the wall, clearing each room. In the main bedroom closet we found an AK rifle. We placed the rifle near the wall we had recently jumped over so that we could pick it up later when we returned to our lines.

We continued our search into other nearby homes, continuing to clear each one room by room. We searched about four houses and were able to find a total of three AK rifles with ammunition. The houses we had just searched were all abandoned. After the search, we grabbed all the recovered rifles and headed back to our observation post. The firearms were then strategically placed in the house we occupied with the idea that they could be used as additional defense should insurgents attack our position. Sgt Shane said, "If we get attacked, no one is running. We will fight until the last man."

After hearing what Sgt Shane said, I thought that it was kind of foolish. Why should we fight until the last man, when we had an entire platoon of Marines and the support of an entire battalion around us? I could see where he was coming from; however, I did not go to Iraq to die "until the last man." I figured if we were close to being overrun, we would hold off the insurgents long enough until reinforcements arrived.

The following week, our team was asked by higher command to set up a blocking position for a 7th Marines battalion, just on the outskirts of Fallujah. We set up our hide position in a two-story house in the middle of a field surrounded by grass and sporadic vegetation. The building was also adjacent to a main road leading into the area where the battalion was set to assault. The battalion would attack an enemy infested neighborhood and our mission was to ambush any fighters going into or out of the area. Our post was set up so that we had 360-degree coverage of the field and the road leading up to the suspected enemy positions.

In our possession, our team had an AK-74 medium machine gun with a drum of ammunition. The machine gun had been confiscated at some point during the battle for Fallujah and Sgt Shane was somehow able to get ahold of it for our use. The idea behind having the weapon was for defensive use should our position come under attack during the main assault. We wanted some extra fire power aside from single shot sniper rifles or the smaller caliber M-16s we had.

On the radio I could hear that the battalion from the 7th Marines was preparing to go into the Fallujah neighborhood. The unit was waiting on the Cobra attack helicopter for air support. When the gunship arrived, the battalion initiated their assault. About a mile down the road from our position, I could hear the battle begin. Rifles and machine guns were barking off from both sides, followed by tank rounds from the battalion. "Roger, we have two enemy snipers firing from the two-story building to your north," I heard one of the Marines report over the radio. The battle continued with increasing ferocity and intensity.

The firing and explosions became more constant while yelling from the battlefield was heard from our post. About a minute after the last transmission I heard on the radio, "Both enemy snipers have been eliminated." It was almost unbelievable to hear the chaos from the noise of the attack, coupled with what sounded like complete professionalism from the Marine force. The neighborhood battle lasted for what seemed like maybe an hour and the Marines came out on top. From what I recall, I do not believe they took any KIA, killed in action, and it sounded like they achieved their objective in clearing out the enemy fighters.

After supporting the Fallujah neighborhood attack, our team would then transfer to 3rd Battalion 4th Marines Lima Company's position along the railroad tracks on the north side of Fallujah. We arrived at their headquarters with their commanding officer by Humvee during the afternoon. Once we arrived, it became obvious that Lima Company had been in a fight. Several of their Marines were wounded and some of them were walking around with bandages wrapped around their heads. Lima Company had been continuously bombarded by rockets and mortars, likely due to their exposed positions near the train tracks.

As we spoke with Lima Company Marines near the outside of their headquarters, we heard an incoming mortar. Everyone within hearing distance ran for cover. The round landed near one of the

## 10. Halting the Advance

Humvees; however, no one was injured or killed. After the area was deemed safe, Sgt Shane and I made our way into their headquarters building. Some Marines who had been wounded were resting and others were simply relaxing.

Sgt Shane and I then met with Lima Company's Gunnery Sergeant who explained to us the current situation. He also showed us which defensive positions the Marines held and from where they were taking insurgent fire. The Gunnery Sergeant also mentioned how many of the town's "citizens" were observing their lines and were likely reporting information back to the enemy fighters.

# 11

# On the Hunt

Later that day while outside of Lima Company's headquarters, I heard a burst of machine gun fire followed by a loud female scream. Apparently, a vehicle with a family inside it failed to yield to a nearby Marine checkpoint. The possibility of a vehicle borne improvised explosive device driving through Lima Company's lines was always a present danger during the battle. There was likely a miscommunication on the part of the Iraqi family because signs were posted in Arabic that were used to notify oncoming cars of the checkpoint. If a vehicle sped up or did not stop for the post, then Marines would have no choice but to defend themselves from a possible attack. Vehicles laden with explosives and going off at coalition checkpoints were not an uncommon occurrence during the war in Iraq.

We had received news from the Marines of Lima Company that one of their guys had been killed earlier that week. His name was Lcpl Tony Graham. I had heard that Graham and another Marine from Lima Company were told to climb onto a tower near Lima Company's position. Both Marines then made their way to the top of the tower by ladder and onto an exposed platform. Once they were in their position, an insurgent sniper began shooting at them from one of the buildings on the outskirts of Fallujah. Graham was then fatally shot, and the other Marine was wounded. Both Marines were eventually recovered from their exposed position on the tower.

As the battle wore on that week, squads from our battalion were being sent off to eat hot food at the Camp Fallujah mess hall. The battle had slowed down and I'm sure higher command thought it would be a good morale booster for members of the battalion to take a break

## 11. On the Hunt

from the lines. When our team got word to go to the hall, it was a nice relief. Mason and I then hitched a ride with a squad from Kilo Company to go eat. Our contingent that went to the base was still wearing the combat gear we wore from the front lines in the city.

When we arrived, we waited in line until we eventually made our way into the chow hall. The majority of the Marines that were present were clean shaven and wore neat utility uniforms. These Marines likely worked on the base itself and were apparently not directly involved in the battle that was taking place nearby. The Kilo Company squad, and I, who had come from the city, had long hair by Marine Corps standards and our uniforms were dirty. I kind of got the feeling that the other Marines inside of the chow hall were looking at us like, "What were these guys into?"

I must admit that I felt some disdain for the Marines who were stationed on Camp Fallujah and were wearing clean uniforms. I was thinking that here we are fighting while they receive the amenities of a well-supplied base. However, I knew I chose the MOS that I was in, and they chose theirs. I couldn't blame them. They had a job to do which was just as important and it was not their fault where they were stationed. Also, many Marines who were considered "POGs" saw more combat than many of the grunts assigned to line companies, in particular the Motor Transport units. They were the ones taking many of the IED attacks as well as the small arms ambushes.

While at Camp Fallujah, I had some time to speak with other members of Kilo Company who had been previously ordered to attack a smaller area just outside of the city. Marines from Kilo Company attacked the area of Karma, which was northeast of the main battle taking place. The attack may have been directed due to the possibility of insurgent fighters fleeing to that specific town. By attacking there, this would likely disrupt the insurgents' ability to regroup and mount counter attacks from that location. One of the Marines who participated in that action described the experience as a tough fight. Tracers could be seen exchanged from both sides, as well as the RPGs fired by the insurgents.

During the Battle for Fallujah, news had circulated that Cpl Dunham, the Marine Corporal who had been assigned to our battalion

## Deployment II: Operation Iraqi Freedom II

prior to his transfer to the 7th Marines, had been killed in Iraq. He had jumped on a grenade that was thrown at his position by an insurgent to save the lives of his fellow Marines. He would be the first Marine since Vietnam to be awarded the Medal of Honor and the second recipient of the medal during the Iraq War (*https://en.wikipedia.org/wiki/Jason_Dunham*). It was an honor to have served with him.

Sgt Shane and our team would return to Lima Company's position on the outskirts of Fallujah in the area of the train station, north of the city later that week. The assault on Fallujah had ceased earlier that day. It was mid-afternoon when we could hear the Iraqi defenders of the city cheering and honking the horns in their vehicles. I looked through the binoculars that I had with me. I saw a white truck filled with what appeared to be Iraqi men and the front passenger was leaning out the of the window holding a large Iraqi flag. He was waving the flag and cheering as the truck drove west along the road adjacent to the edge of the city. It appeared that the defenders believed that they had won the battle and successfully defended their city.

The 3rd Battalion 4th Marines Scout/Sniper platoon consolidated on the outskirts of Fallujah as the unit was preparing to completely remove itself from the city. We were met by our battalion commander Lt Col McConnel. He told us how the Marine Command Staff met with Iraqi leadership and what terms were being discussed to bring a conclusion to the battle. The Iraqis mentioned that they wanted three elements removed from the city: the AC-130 gunships, the tanks, and Marine Scout/Snipers. Lt Col McConnel was satisfied with our platoon's effectiveness during the battle and told us that the non–school trained PIGs should be given the official title of 8541. I did not feel too comfortable with that idea even though I had actually performed the job in combat. Needless to say, that prospect would not come to be and rightfully so.

The 3rd Battalion 4th Marines would then return to the Haditha Dam where the deployment had started. It was mid–April 2004, when we were eating our dinner on the top level of the operating base. At this time, Marcus, who was a member of our platoon on another team, was speaking with one of the motor transport Marines while we stood around and ate. The Marine from motor transport told us about

## 11. On the Hunt

a recent ambush along one of the MSRs in Iraq. He said that they were driving along the road when they came under heavy insurgent fire. "It was raining bullets sideways," the Marine said to describe the attack on their convoy. During the ambush, Lt Jimenez, their platoon leader, had been shot in the head while in one of the convoy vehicles.

As we performed our observation posts around the Haditha area, Sgt Shane came up with the idea of blending in with the population to help find and kill the insurgents placing the IEDs near the MSRs. Sgt Shane was able to get an old late '80s model Iraqi vehicle for the mission. It was a cheap and boxy looking red four-seater car. The front and rear seats were removed to allow one of our Marines to lie in the prone position inside the passenger compartment. This would then allow him to take the shot through the trunk. In order to do this, a small port was cut into the thin metal of the trunk which then created a small metal flap. The bottom portion of the metal flap was left attached to the vehicle which could then be pulled back by a cord held by the shooter or observer. Once the port was open, there was maybe a window of five inches by five inches for the shooter to take the shot without penetrating the trunk.

In addition to our "blending in," our team wore shemagh scarfs and Iraqi thawbs, and we would carry AK rifles instead of our standard M-16s. We would also have our .50 caliber SASR in the vehicle as well. The IEDs were the battalion's top concern at that time and the idea of catching insurgents placing roadside bombs became a real possibility. The car that Sgt Shane was able to get was somewhat clean looking. He got the idea that if he somehow made the car look dirtier, we would be less conspicuous; therefore, he covered the vehicle in dirt.

Our first undercover mission was to be a reconnaissance on the roads just outside of Haditha city. The team dressed in the Iraqi garb with head wraps and AK rifles. We loaded up into the red Iraqi car and headed toward the outskirts of the town. As we drove off from the base, we radioed in our departure to battalion headquarters. It was about 4:00 p.m. at the time we left the Haditha Dam. It was still kind of hot and the flak jackets that we wore under the thawbs made it that much more uncomfortable.

# Deployment II: Operation Iraqi Freedom II

**Our attempt at blending in with the Iraqi population in Haditha, Iraq (April 2004).**

The reconnaissance conducted that evening was rather uneventful; however, it appeared that we were undetected by the civilian and insurgent population. We scouted the surrounding roads just outside of the town until we eventually set up along one of the MSRs leading to the dam. Our team scanned the area for several hours; however, we did not observe any insurgents placing IEDs into the nearby roadways. We eventually drove off and returned to base.

The following day, we would return and scout the outer roads surrounding the city of Haditha. As we traveled along one of the MSRs leading away from the area, we noticed an Iraqi truck following our car. The truck was driven by an Iraqi man and the bed of the vehicle was loaded with Iraqi males. The truck eventually tailed our car at which time Sgt Shane told Dean and me to start shooting at them with our AK rifles. We were unsure as to who they were, but we thought they might be insurgents that somehow knew we were Americans

## 11. On the Hunt

scouting the area. Dean and I were initially hesitant to fire on the truck; however, the vehicle full of Iraqi men did not let up. "Shoot at the motherfuckers!" yelled Sgt Shane.

Dean then placed his body partially out of the passenger window of our car and fired several AK rounds at the Iraqi vehicle. The truck's driver then immediately applied his brakes as we were then able to gain some distance. I got on the radio and requested for QRF at a designated rally point. We advised QRF that our mission was compromised, and we needed immediate extraction. I also told QRF that we were being tailed by possible enemy insurgents and gave a description of their truck. Our team reached the rally point within about five minutes. The extraction team then reached our position shortly thereafter.

Once we returned to base, Sgt Shane decided that it was too dangerous to drive around Haditha in Iraqi garb. We later learned from the QRF team that the people on the Iraqi truck that followed our team were Haditha citizens who thought we were the "Mujahedeen" or insurgents as the American military referred to them. They were Iraqi citizens who were trying to rid their town of what they thought were terrorists. I was surprised at this revelation because I thought that most of the Haditha population was against the American occupation.

Sgt Shane and our team would continue to conduct reconnaissance missions along the MSRs around Haditha Dam. This would be done for weeks until one day we received intelligence that an artillery round which had been wired as an IED was found in an old shed near one of the roads leading toward the base. The artillery round was partially converted into an IED and appeared to be pre-staged for roadside placement. With this knowledge, our team decided to set up an observation post near the shed to see who might pick up the artillery round and ambush them if necessary.

With the discovery of the IED, Sgt Shane and our team set up near the shed later that evening. We would get in position near the side of the road without issue. Our post was set up about fifty yards from the structure and we were able to keep sight on it, should anyone pick up the IED. As the night went on, I eventually fell asleep while Sgt Shane remained on watch.

What felt like shortly after falling asleep I heard, "Brian, get up!"

## Deployment II: Operation Iraqi Freedom II

Sgt Shane said in a loud whisper. "Someone is grabbing the IED!" I looked up toward the road where the storage shed was located that held the wired artillery round. As I looked over, I heard the engine of a semi-truck start, and I could see the headlights then turn on. I quickly threw my ammunition satchel over my neck and shoulder while grabbing my rifle. The M-16 I had was equipped with a M240-grenade launcher. From my understanding, whoever arrived in the semi-truck was there for the IED.

The semi-truck began making its way down the MSR which was adjacent to our observation post. I then ran toward the dirt berm overlooking the road with my aforementioned gear. By the time I reached the berm, the truck was almost alongside where I was standing. I aimed my rifle at the windshield area of the truck and then began shooting, hoping to the stop the driver from leaving with the IED. I was maybe fifteen to twenty yards from the vehicle when I fired off an entire magazine of thirty rounds. I then launched a round from the grenade launcher that was already loaded in the chamber. Upon impact of the round, the fuel tank immediately caught fire and quickly began engulfing the passenger compartment of the semi as it rolled down the street. I could hear what sounded like several men screaming inside of the truck.

The yelling was horrible to hear. It sounded like they were being burned alive and their voices carried in the quiet calm of the late desert night. I ran from the berm and back to my position to consolidate for extraction. I was shaking and trying to gather myself after what just happened. After ambushing the semi-truck, we called for the QRF to come to our post. Our team was eventually taken out of the area and returned to the Haditha Dam for debrief.

The following week, our team conducted a combined observation post mission with Sgt Wright from the other Scout/Sniper section within our platoon. We headed out in the evening as usual under the cover of darkness and were dropped off at our designated point. Our combined team of four men patrolled from the drop-off point and moved into position overlooking a small neighborhood in Haditha. The plan was to stay in the observation post for two days and then extract out of the area. The purpose of the mission was to prevent

## 11. On the Hunt

IED emplacement along the MSR near the town. The evening after our insertion was uneventful as members of the team continuously switched out on the optics for systematic observation.

The evening turned into day as the cold of the night transitioned to heat from the late morning sun. As we sat in our dugout, Sgt Shane pointed out a nearby goat herder walking about a hundred and fifty yards away from our position. It was a single male herder with a group of approximately ten to fifteen goats. All the members of our team immediately ducked our heads below the dirt line to avoid detection. We lay on our backs for several minutes as we could hear the herd travel closer. We lay there as quietly as possible as we then heard the bell attached to one of the goat's necks as it got closer.

I could then hear the bell as if it was almost on top of our position, followed up by the shadow of a small goat overlapping the nearby dirt wall. Some of us tried to contain our laughter as we saw more goats stand at the edge of our observation post, while simply chewing away at some food in their mouths. We then heard the voice of the herder as he tried to rally the animals toward him. The man soon walked up on our position and we immediately stood up and grabbed our gear. We knew our position was compromised and we just quickly walked away to our extraction point.

Yet again our team would be assigned to another mission as the weeks carried on. We would be attached to a task force that would be part of a raid on a suspected insurgent house. The task force was comprised mostly of Marines from our battalion with an Army Special Forces team known as Operational Detachment Alpha or ODA. The briefing for the raid took place in the afternoon on top of the Haditha Dam. Our team was to provide cover on the rooftop of the target house to keep a counterattack at bay. The Marines involved in the task force loaded up into their Humvees and prepared to move out.

The task force was comprised of approximately twenty-five Marines in five Humvees. The raid would take place in the town of Haditha in the middle of the night when the inhabitants of the suspected insurgent house would likely be sleeping. As the contingent traveled out of the base that evening, members of the party conducted

## Deployment II: Operation Iraqi Freedom II

their usual radio checks and ensured everyone was ready to go. The task force then drove off base and headed into town under the cover of darkness.

Our team was linked with a detachment from Kilo Company. As we got closer to the target location inside of town, I could hear the Weapons Company Gunnery Sergeant, who was part of the task force, on the radio and giving updates on the situation. The Weapons Company Gunnery Sergeant oversaw the CAAT (Combined Anti-Armor Team) team assigned to the raid party and then stated on the radio, "You have a squad size of males running from the building! Cut them off!" Just as we heard the Gunnery Sergeant over the radio, our Humvees raced across the bridge leading into town in order to get the raid started and to prevent the previously seen Iraqi males from setting up an ambush.

The Humvees from the task force then set up around the target house and the Marines exited the vehicles to get in their positions. No contact was made with the group of Iraqi males because they had apparently fled the area. Our team hurried toward the target house as we rushed to get to the rooftop. We walked along a small wall running alongside the house leading to the upper level. It was nearly pitch-black outside, and I had lost my footing as I tried to balance on the small wall. With my full gear, I fell backward and onto a large wooden crate hugging the house. The crack of the wood was rather loud as I hurried to get back onto my feet.

I quickly returned with my team as we eventually made our way to the rooftop. Once in position, the raid began. The Operational Detachment Alpha team with an attachment of Marines made entry into the target building. I heard what sounded like two shots from a rifle inside of the home, followed by yelling. I then heard the detachment order people to the ground as the house was being cleared. The mission would be completed without friendly casualties.

When we exited our position that morning for debrief, I learned that the shots fired from inside the target location came from one of the Army Special Forces soldiers. When they made entry into the home, an Iraqi had grabbed an AK rifle which had then been literally shot out of his hands with what was known as a "double tap," which is

## 11. On the Hunt

two shots fired in rapid succession. Whether or not the Special Operator meant to do that was never really made clear.

My battalion would soon return to the United States from its second Iraq War deployment in late summer of 2004. Returning home again to the United States was a great feeling. Arriving at the Twenty-Nine Palms Marine Corps base was also exhilarating. Friends and family members awaited our return to the field of the base recreational park. People were cheering and yelling for joy when our buses approached their gathering. Some of the friends and family had signs welcoming their loved ones. It was a very good feeling to see so much support. As the buses pulled into the parking lot near the field, I could see my family and wife Stephanie. I had not seen my wife in the United States for about a year and a half.

Up to that point in my life, I had never been so happy and grateful. I was home, I was alive, and my wife was there to greet me. Life was good to say the least. I had never felt so alive, and it seemed like everything was perfect, almost like a movie. The emotions that day were very high, and it was amazing to see so many friends. As I got off the bus, Stephanie ran up to me and gave me a big kiss. We then just hugged each other tightly as we told one another how much we loved and missed one other. I then hugged my parents and sisters who were waiting nearby. My mom was very emotional and was crying tears of joy.

After greeting everyone, my family and I went to the house that Stephanie had rented for us just outside of the base. It was a small, but comfortable home because anything was an improvement from the living conditions that I experienced in Iraq. We simply relaxed for a while and continued to talk some more. I could tell that my family was excited to spend time with me; however, I could also sense that they just wanted to leave Stephanie and me alone. My family would eventually go home so that my wife and I could catch up for the rest of the day.

While back home, as several days passed, I noticed that Stephanie and her male Army friend had become very close since their Iraq deployment. One day while discussing her time overseas, she had admitted to taking a shower in front of this male friend. She then told

## Deployment II: Operation Iraqi Freedom II

me he was the one who poured water on her from the top of her transport vehicle because that was the only way they could shower when none were available. I asked, "So he poured water on you and saw you naked?!" She replied yes and that it was no big deal because it meant nothing.

I was very upset after hearing that some other guy had seen my wife in that way. To make matters more difficult she also hung a photo of herself with her Army friend in the hallway of our house. Again, she insisted nothing happened between them and that he was like the "gay friend." One day when my sisters visited me at my house, they brought up the photo of Stephanie and her friend in the hallway. They felt the photo was inappropriate and that it should not be in my house. I agreed and told them Stephanie's reasoning.

The photo of her Army friend would lead to arguments that one day were brought to a head. We were in our house when I became so upset, I slammed the photo on the countertop, smashing out the glass from the frame. I had enough of seeing her friend displayed that way in my own home and did not wait almost two years to see her, only to have our relationship disrespected in that manner. She insisted that I was overreacting; however, I did not care about her view at that point.

While I was back in the United States, the Second Battle of Fallujah took place in November of 2004. I saw portions of the battle take place while watching the news with my family back home. I told my family that I should be there, and it bothered me that I was unable to participate in that operation. The timing of the second battle seemed to coincide with then United States President George W. Bush securing his second term in the White House.

Word came down from the 3rd Battalion 4th Marines higher command that our unit would eventually deploy back to Iraq for a third tour. Leaving for my third Iraq deployment was tough because Stephanie and I had separated. I was already weary due to the close calls on my last two deployments and here I was going on deployment number three. Again, what would I encounter? Would this deployment be tougher than the others or would it be easier? Prior to every deployment I wondered if I would survive and that was always a heavy

## 11. On the Hunt

feeling. However, I always did my best to stay optimistic about going overseas.

A few weeks prior to my third deployment to Iraq, my dad came to visit me from Idaho. We then met up with my brother in Palmdale for dinner and drinks at a local Mexican restaurant. After eating, we ordered some Cadillac margaritas and got intoxicated. The deployment had still been on my mind and drinking the alcohol did not really help with the emotions I had felt at that time. After the dinner and drinks, we ended up back at my parents' house in Palmdale. My brother and I got a ride from the restaurant from a friend.

As my brother and I got out of the car, it hit me that this was the last time we would see each other prior to the deployment. In my intoxicated state, my emotions came out. I hugged my brother and told him I was concerned about going back to Iraq. I knew that with my previous two deployments there were close calls on my life, and I knew that with every combat deployment anything could happen. He told me not to worry as we walked into my parents' house to get some rest.

# Deployment III: Operation Iraqi Freedom III
*(February to August 2005)*

# 12

# Returning to Fallujah

My battalion loaded up into the 7-ton transport trucks as we awaited departure to Camp Fallujah from a coalition airbase in northern Iraq. The battalion was to leave late in the evening under the cover of darkness. Upon leaving base, the trucks traveled along the MSR leading toward Fallujah. Marines were sitting in the back of the 7-tons outfitted with only the overhead tarp covers. The sides of the transport vehicles were completely open. Apparently the MSR leading up to Fallujah was deemed safe enough for military travel since the Second Battle of Fallujah destroyed a large enemy contingent in the area.

Traveling along the road would take the entire evening. It was very cold, and the added wind chill felt from sitting in the rear of an open 7-ton truck did not help. I wore what I could to stay warm, from my Gore-Tex jacket to gloves. It did not seem to matter; it was so cold that my body started to shiver with what felt like no hope of getting warmer. There was really nothing one could do other than just sit there and hope we would arrive at Camp Fallujah soon.

The wind chill did not let up as I tried my best to take a nap. It got so cold that at one point I thought I might not wake up if I fell asleep. A part of me was hoping for an ambush so that I would have a reason to get out of the truck and move around. I had never been so cold in my life. To make matters worse, I had to pee; however, I obviously had to hold it for what seemed like a long time.

Once we finally arrived at Camp Fallujah, I hurried off the 7-ton truck so that I could find a spot to urinate. I had been holding my pee for most of the ride and I was not going to wait around to use a port-a-john or restroom. I then quickly found a small trailer to relieve

## Deployment III: Operation Iraqi Freedom III

myself behind. My hands were so numb that at that point, I could barely move my fingers to unzip my trousers. I rushed to open my zipper and partially urinated on my pants because I could barely feel my hands.

Later that day, my Scout/Sniper section met with the snipers from the 1st Battalion 3rd Marines (1/3). This Marine Corps unit had fought in the Second Battle of Fallujah and had been engaged in extensive combat when the operation took place. At this time, we looked over tactical maps of the city of Fallujah in our company tent. The snipers from 1/3 were telling my team where they had fought in the battle in regards to the map and how many enemy combatants each of their snipers had killed.

The Scout Leader from 1/3 mentioned that each sniper in their platoon had killed approximately twenty insurgents each. One of the other snipers at the table mentioned having withdrawals from not shooting any more enemy combatants. I looked over at him and thought, "How much combat did these guys see?!" I had a feeling they had been through a lot, and I was eager to learn from their experiences.

For us to complete our designated mission in Fallujah, we had to review and become familiar with our Area of Operations within the city. The 3/4 India Company replaced the positions that a company from 1/3 had held within the city after the battle. My sniper team was paired up with another sniper team from 1/3 where we conducted a "left seat, right seat." The aforementioned term is used to refer to our shadowing of the other sniper teams to become familiar with their positions and the tactics they used to operate post-battle. This was similar to what our unit had done when we replaced the Army unit in Haditha the year prior.

We would enter the city from Camp Fallujah on Humvees. It appeared that every single building there had either been demolished or had some type of munition impact from the Second Battle of Fallujah. No building was left unscathed. I specifically recall a business building along one of the MSRs in the city that had what appeared to be .50 caliber bullet impacts in the room of the second floor.

Near the impacts was a large spray of blood where an insurgent most likely had been ripped apart by the rounds. It was an eerie feeling

## 12. Returning to Fallujah

seeing so much destruction and the aftermath of the battle. As we continued along the MSR and toward one of the outposts, one of the snipers from 1/3 pointed out a skeleton along the road in a ditch. It was either an Iraqi civilian or enemy combatant from the battle, but there was really no way to know for sure.

We arrived at the forward operating base located within the southern portion of Fallujah. The Marines from 1/3 still occupied much of the base which was a large abandoned Iraqi home. As we walked around the inside of the building, many of the doors had the names of Marines killed during the battle that were written in black marker. There would be three names on one door, then maybe four more names on another. This type of writing was seen throughout several doors of the forward operating bases occupied by Marines from the Second Battle of Fallujah. Looking at the ranks of the Marines listed as KIA on the doors, I would assume most of the ones killed were likely late teens or early twenties.

It was almost an uncomfortable feeling being around the Marines from 1/3 from having seen a glimpse of what they went through. It was obvious to me that they had fought a tough battle, and it was an honor to be there hearing their stories. One of the snipers from 1/3 mentioned that it seemed like there was a call for a medevac over the radio constantly. The sniper also mentioned that their Marines had been consistently taking casualties as they cleared buildings; therefore, if there was any suspicion of enemy fighters in any structure, a U.S. armored bulldozer would knock it down. He added that the insurgents had Chechen fighters incorporated into their defending force during the battle. The Chechen snipers would deliberately fire at the soft spots in the Marines' flak vests to bypass the protective ceramic plates.

That afternoon, while at another one of the Forward Operating Bases within Fallujah, the Chief Scout from 1/3 Scout/Snipers noted something about our team. While sitting down with his back up against a wall, he looked up and said, "It's funny how well you guys get along. After a few months of being here and seeing each other all the time, you are all going to get on each other's nerves." We kind of laughed at his remark, but I already knew how true that was from

## Deployment III: Operation Iraqi Freedom III

previous deployments. Our team did get along well, and I hoped it would stay that way for the sake of getting through our stay in Iraq.

Our team would initially be attached to India Company 3/4. A platoon from India Company would take over a small factory previously used by 1/3 as a forward outpost within Fallujah. The factory itself was run down and it appeared to have not been in use for some time. Our team's living quarters would consist of a small room hugging the main factory building, about twenty feet by ten feet. The room was not luxurious by any means; however, it was a solid roof over our heads and was more private than what we were used to from our last deployment.

Many of the missions that would take place from India Company's base would be observation posts. Just as in the previous deployment, our team focused on providing overwatch on roads in Fallujah in the middle of the night to prevent IED emplacement. The city was pitch black due to the lack of electrical power in the buildings and streets. It was a ghost town where a lot of people had recently died in violent fashion.

About two weeks later, we mounted India Company's Humvees from their operating base in preparation for a night observation post inside of Fallujah. The post was to be set on a rooftop in the dense industrial sector in the southwest portion of the city. Two other Humvees were being loaded up by India Company Marines with a security element for our insertion. The security element would not accompany my team on the mission and was only there should we come under fire during drop-off.

As my team initially got onto the rooftop position, we all heard a loud potshot ring out through the near pitch-black neighborhood. The shock that we might be getting ambushed raced through my mind; however, we heard no other shots. Our team sat there listening for any other signs of possible enemy activity. The security element from India Company had already left the area and my heart rate had soared in response to the unexpected noise. My adrenaline was pumping as it was eerily quiet in the dark neighborhood. There was dense cloud cover overhead as well which made the area even darker from the lack of moonlight illumination.

## 12. Returning to Fallujah

After reassuring ourselves that there was no ambush, we conducted two-hour shifts between our four-man team. The team consisted of myself, Marcus, two other Scout/Sniper platoon members: Hank and Travis. It was very windy, and it felt like thirty degrees that night. The wind was blowing hard and fast as I tried to sleep after my shift. I eventually fell asleep; however, I would occasionally wake up to the wind chill penetrating my feet through my sleeping bag.

Early the following morning, a security detachment from India Company returned to our position with about three Humvees. We immediately grabbed our gear and ran downstairs to meet with the extraction team. We then loaded up in the last Humvee of the small convoy. The team sat down in the rear of the open top vehicle with my pack still on my back. The extraction team then drove westward along the road leading away from the building we just occupied and toward India Company's forward operating base. The Humvees drove for approximately one mile until the calm of the dark early morning was interrupted by the crack of several AK rifle potshots in rapid succession. The firing sounded like it came from the buildings adjacent to the road on our north side, and the realization that we were caught in an ambush set in.

I immediately dropped from my seat and onto the bed of the Humvee seeking immediate protection from the steel plates that surrounded our vehicle. Most of my body had been exposed to the nearby rooftops and the last thing that I wanted was to catch an AK round to the face or chest. Marcus, who had been sitting across from me, had immediately turned around while returning fire with several other Marines into random buildings where they believed the fire was coming from. My pack had restricted the movement of my arms, and it would have been very difficult to shoulder my rifle. I was facing northward when the ambush started, and I saw what appeared to be a round impact the rear of the Humvee armor. There was a large spark from where the munition had struck.

Our convoy sped through the kill zone as quickly as possible. The Humvees eventually pulled over onto an open lot area about a mile from where the ambush occurred. Some Marines wanted to go back in and continue the fight. Other Marines including myself figured that

## Deployment III: Operation Iraqi Freedom III

was what the insurgents wanted, and it would have led to a trap. It was eventually decided to return to base because no one knew exactly where the enemy was within the ambush area.

Conducting observation posts within the city of Fallujah at night was always an eerie undertaking. Most of the city was in ruins from the recent battle that took place and there were no streetlights to illuminate the neighborhoods. It appeared to be a vast, dark wasteland of destroyed buildings and homes.

The following month during midafternoon when my team was resting, I was lying on a mat in an industrial building occupied by India Company in Fallujah. The room was very dark when suddenly, I felt my body lift up off of the ground accompanied by the sound of a massive explosion. You would have thought the building would have collapsed with the shock wave of the detonation. I could hear one of the squad leaders from India Company shouting, "Grab your shit! Man your posts!" Marines were frantically running around believing that the building was under insurgent attack. We would later find out that the explosion was American EOD (Explosive Ordnance Disposal) conducting a controlled detonation nearby.

It was a sad sight to see how the Iraqi citizens were coping with the destruction of their homes after the battles for Fallujah. During our patrols of the inner portion of the city, I would see families living out of destroyed homes while trying to scratch out an existence. For whatever side they took during the previous battles, it was pretty amazing to see the positivity displayed by some of the Iraqi children as we passed by during our foot patrols. Many would say hi and most of them wanted something from us. We would pass out candy or whatever items we felt like giving to the kids.

On one instance, I recall conducting a patrol from Kilo Company's forward operating base within Fallujah. A few Iraqi kids approached our squad as we patrolled the streets. The kids said, "Mister, Mister!" and would then put their hands out in hopes of receiving something, anything it seemed like. At this time, I pulled out my hand sanitizer and one child who was maybe seven years old immediately reached for the bottle in my hand. He was able to grab it as I tightened my grip around the sanitizer. The child struggled very hard to take

## 12. Returning to Fallujah

the bottle and his face said it all. His young face showed desperation and he was absolutely determined to have it. I loosened my grip on the item and the child quickly snatched it away.

It was wearing to be continuously around so much destruction. To constantly see these Iraqi families trying to manage some sort of living through rubble with little to no electrical power. I would continuously think to myself on the foot patrols in the city of Fallujah of how much I wanted to return home and go to college. To earn that better life for myself because those opportunities were there. The people that I saw, the Iraqi citizens in the city of Fallujah, did not have that opportunity. It seemed like there would be no hope for their lives to get better anytime soon and I think many of them knew that.

The weeks continued to go by. At one point Travis and I stood on the rooftop of the combined American-Iraqi forward outpost in Fallujah. We were talking when suddenly a huge explosion about 400 yards

**An Iraqi family greeting us while on foot patrol through the city of Fallujah (April 2005).**

## Deployment III: Operation Iraqi Freedom III

from our position practically lifted me off my feet. The detonation was extremely loud as I then noticed a large almost mushroom cloud–like plume. "What the hell was that?!" I initially thought. Then it crossed my mind that it may have been a VBIED that exploded prematurely. Information came over the radio that it was a controlled detonation conducted by an American Explosive Ordnance team. That shock and adrenaline rush that caused my heart to race many times before was again felt surging throughout my body. "Well thanks for letting us know after the fact!" I thought.

On one specific afternoon in the city, I recall going into one of the nearby Iraqi Army barracks to meet with some of their leadership for an upcoming operation. The moment our team walked into their makeshift residential barracks; I could sense their anger as they looked at us. I glanced around and could see many of the Iraqi soldiers looking at us with hate. It was obvious that many of them did not like us because we were Americans. There was little doubt in my mind that many of the Iraqi soldiers were playing both sides. Regardless, we as Americans would have to do our best to work with them with hopes that one day they would take over military operations against the insurgency.

About halfway into my third deployment, word came down to my Scout/Sniper section that we would participate in a combined Scout/Sniper task force. The mission was to provide overwatch along the roads leading toward Camp Fallujah, due to coalition convoys coming under recent IED attacks. Travis and I would travel with a three vehicle AAV convoy one afternoon as it traveled along the MSR leading up to Fallujah. At that time, I had my head out of the top hatch while looking around for possible observation positions from the rear of the AAV.

While looking around, I glanced over at the Amtrack directly behind mine when the AAV in trail was suddenly hit by an IED. "Oh fuck! The track behind us just got hit!" I yelled down to Travis in the track after I saw the explosion. The convoy then halted and set up in a defensive perimeter. Word came back over the radio that the Marines in the track that got hit were unharmed, just shaken up. The reactive armor along the side of the AAV must have absorbed most of the impact.

## 12. Returning to Fallujah

**A photograph of allied Iraqi soldiers and me at a post in Fallujah (April 2005).**

Several Marines then exited some of the AAVs. About three Marines approached a nearby shop where an Iraqi teenage boy was standing and looking around. One Marine grabbed him and immediately tripped him to the ground. It was likely they thought that the Iraqi boy was involved in the IED attack because of where the shop was positioned in relation to the explosion. It was not uncommon for the insurgents setting off the IEDs to have spotters. It also would not have been uncommon for the boy to have set off the IED with a simple cell phone.

After the scouting mission, we returned to Camp Fallujah. As our team walked around the headquarters area, we were approached by a Marine captain who was attached to the task force. "Hey guys, where did you shoot that guy with the shovel?" said the captain. We did not know who he was and did not know what he was talking about. I assumed he thought that we were a different Scout/Sniper team that had killed an insurgent. "Which guy?" Travis said. "The guy digging on

### Deployment III: Operation Iraqi Freedom III

the side of the road," replied the Marine captain. He then mentioned that it must have been a different team because we had not shot any insurgents during our time so far with the task force.

Later in the evening, Travis and I were picked up by a Humvee team attached to the aforementioned operation. They were our insertion team. We loaded up our gear and introduced ourselves to the driver as well as the passenger. Our team then exited Camp Fallujah under the cover of darkness as Travis and I explained where our observation location would be. During the middle of our conversation, the driver of the Humvee thanked us for what we were doing. The road we would watch had been continually planted with IEDs and he may have encountered many during his tour in Iraq. He seemed genuinely grateful for the mission we were about to conduct.

We were inserted into our observation post area earlier that evening. Travis and I positioned ourselves along an MSR where we would provide IED overwatch for the night. We then set up our post on a

**A destroyed section of Fallujah viewed from an American/Iraqi outpost (April 2005).**

## 12. Returning to Fallujah

large embankment that overlooked that same road. For much of the evening there was minimal traffic along the highway with no suspicious activity. Several hours had passed with Travis and I continuously switching shifts on observing the highway for IED emplacement.

Travis was on watch when he suddenly alerted me to a suspicious Iraqi vehicle that had stopped on the shoulder of the highway. The car engine and lights were then turned off when Travis mentioned that he saw two males exit the vehicle. The males were walking around on the side of the dirt road. I then asked him what they were doing. Travis said that they started to dig in the dirt near the car. To us, that was a clear indicator that they were prepping the roadway for IED placement. It was common practice for insurgents to dig a hole along a highway and have the IED placed in the same hole at a later time. American rules of engagement indicated that anyone digging along the side of a road (coupled with other actions) that was commonly used by coalition military vehicles was fair to engage.

We were in our position for about a minute when we saw the vehicle lights turn on. I told Travis to grab his rifle and that we needed to head down to the edge of the embankment to set up an ambush before they left the area. We both grabbed our M-16s and ran down toward the edge of the road as fast as we could, leaving behind our protective gear. Once we reached the edge of the embankment near the MSR, we both lay flat on the ground and waited for the vehicle to approach.

By the time we got into our position, the Iraqi car was driving in our direction. When the vehicle was about fifteen yards away, I began firing into the car. Travis quickly followed suit. We shot approximately twenty rounds into the car. It was very dark and had been somewhat difficult to aim down the iron sights of my rifle. The car had slowed to a stop, and nothing could be heard from the vehicle. We then immediately ran back to our observation post to radio what just happened to the reaction force. My heart was racing. The adrenaline rush from the ambush had kicked in and it was never a comfortable feeling.

The extraction team responded shortly after to pick us up from our position and to examine the Iraqi vehicle. Once extracted, we met with the task force leader, a young second lieutenant. We were told that the two Iraqi men in the vehicle survived the ambush and that the

## Deployment III: Operation Iraqi Freedom III

car had been set up for detonation. With that knowledge, Travis and I felt we had done the right thing and prevented a future IED that could have been used against coalition forces.

After the task force, there were many other observation post missions to be conducted. One day, Marcus and I had set up an observation post in an old mill complex. We were accompanied by two other Marines from India Company. We cleared the location and set up our position along a wall overlooking an open field near a roadway leading deeper into Fallujah. For most of the day, there was not much vehicle or pedestrian traffic that came through our field of view. It was about mid-afternoon when I was walking around the open compound within the mill.

I was walking with Marcus and one of the security element Marines when we heard a low sounding boom in the distance. Everyone stopped in place and looked around as we tried to decide on what we had just heard. Several seconds passed when we heard the roar of an incoming round. You would have thought a freight train was going

**Allied Iraqi soldiers and me at an outpost (April 2005).**

## 12. Returning to Fallujah

to land on our position. We all then ran for cover as the roar was immediately followed by a loud explosion maybe ten to fifteen yards away, possibly on the nearby street.

After the impact, everyone gave out a nervous laugh as we figured it was either a large mortar round or rocket that had been launched by an insurgent team. We were not sure if any other rounds would come in on our position, so we set up a defensive perimeter within the compound. There was a heightened sense of alertness, and my adrenaline was yet again soaring. My heart was racing as everyone tried to laugh off what had just happened and we scanned our area for any signs of enemy activity. We were slightly anxious, but more focused on whether we would see any insurgent movement nearby or in the distance. About a half hour passed as we continued our scan with no other enemy rounds landing on or near our position.

# 13

# Blue on Blue

It was April of 2005. I was lying in my bed at the battalion headquarters located on Abu Ghraib. It was maybe seven in the morning when Travis walked into our room. He appeared distraught and said, "Jose is gone." Everyone in the room was shocked. Jose belonged to another Scout/Sniper section in my battalion and was a 19-year-old Hispanic kid from Simi Valley, California. Travis then told us that Jose had been in the hospital the night prior and had died from his injuries. When we asked what happened, he mentioned that a Marine Reconnaissance team in their Humvees got lost in our area of operations and mistook Jose's team for a group of insurgents on the side of the road.

After seeing Jose's group, one of the Reconnaissance Humvees turned toward his team and began firing one of their machine guns at them. The Humvee then rushed closer to Jose's position when Jose pushed Gill, who was another member of his team, out of harm's way before he was then struck by the Reconnaissance Humvee. It was also discovered that Jose had been shot. We sat in the room in disbelief when we heard the news about his death. Some of the guys in the room began wiping the tears from their faces as did I. The platoon just lost a good friend, and he was one of the nicest guys I had ever met. Someone we had lived and trained with for over a year was suddenly gone.

The ceremony for Jose would be held in the cafeteria area at the Abu Ghraib base a few days later. His M-16 and bayonet was placed downward on a small platform with his helmet placed on top. His boots were placed in front of his M-16 alongside his M-40 sniper rifle and radio. The cafeteria was lined with metal folding chairs and was

## 13. Blue on Blue

filled with Marines. The battalion chaplain greeted all in attendance followed by a prayer. The chaplain spoke about the kind of man Jose was and how he would be missed. Near the end of the ceremony, the song "Free Bird" by Lynyrd Skynyrd was played as Marines walked past and patted the helmet placed on his rifle as a sign of farewell.

**Jose's display during a commemoration of his life in Abu Ghraib, Iraq (April 2005).**

# Deployment III: Operation Iraqi Freedom III

As I stood near the rear of the cafeteria, I could see a row of Marines in attendance that I had never seen before. I was under the impression that they may have been the Reconnaissance Marines involved in his death. Some of the Reconnaissance Marines were wiping their eyes as the conclusion of the ceremony progressed. I got in line to show my respects to Jose. I did the sign of the cross and patted his helmet. As I walked by his display, I immediately walked out of the cafeteria area and found the nearest room I could to shield myself in. The nearest "room" happened to be a nearby restroom. I quickly walked inside of it and was wiping the tears that began streaming down my face.

When I was sure no one could see me, I immediately cried harder while trying to clear the tears running down my cheeks with the sleeve of my blouse. Our platoon had lost a good friend, and the pain was felt. I eventually made my way back to the battalion cafeteria area where Jose's ceremony took place. I would take photos with members from our platoon in front of Jose's rifle and helmet. After taking several other photos, the platoon gathered near Jose's display and we all hugged, locked arm over shoulder in one big circle. I could hear and feel Marcus crying next to me. It had been difficult to hold back my emotions as we stood there for our friend.

The platoon would carry on without Jose for the remainder of the deployment and we would deal with the loss as best we all could. Several of the guys in the platoon were very close to Jose because they had lived with him and were teammates in his section. It appeared they were taking his death the hardest. I knew Gill was having a difficult time, because Jose helped save his life before losing his own.

Our observation post missions throughout the city of Fallujah would continue after only about two days off to mourn for Jose. The operations throughout the ghost town were monotonous much in the way they were in the previous deployment. Day after day sitting in a single room or building, rotating shifts after several hours. There seemed to always be enough time to replay almost all the past events in my life with additional time to plan ahead.

Hidden posts in the city required more attention to detail in my opinion. There were many more areas to keep an eye out for with little

## 13. Blue on Blue

room for complacency. Any window could hide an enemy sniper. Any Iraqi vehicle could be laying an IED on the side of a road. The thought of being overrun by an insurgent force was always present in my mind. I would think back to the Marine Corps sniper team in Ramadi that had been attacked in their building and were all killed. Due to that incident, it became common practice for my Scout/Sniper platoon to go out on missions with at least four men, most of the time.

It was common knowledge that the Iraqi insurgents despised coalition force snipers. The sniper's world was well suited to the cat and mouse warfare that we found ourselves in during this war. It was rare that the enemy combatants would remain for a standup fight against the Americans. The attacks usually came in the form of roadside bombs or small-arms ambushes, after which the insurgents would quickly assimilate back into the population.

As the completion of the third deployment drew nearer, my team would be tasked with overwatch on a municipal building in the heart of Fallujah. A local Iraqi election was taking place, and my team would enter a building that overlooked the highway that ran through the middle of the city. Our team made its way into the multi-story building where we were met by a small Iraqi family. The family was in the hallway near the main entrance of the structure. Our team was clearing a portion of the building when one of the security element Marines, who had been attached to our section, told an elderly lady of the family, "Get the fuck out of here!" as he motioned toward the main entrance.

"Hello?! Get the fuck out of here!" as the Marine continued to motion toward the entrance. I looked on with disgust. No wonder some of these people hate us, I thought as the Marine shooed the elderly woman away. I tried to imagine how I would have felt had that been my family member and what I would have felt if she told me that some soldier from another country forced her out of her own home. Our team would eventually clear out the rest of the structure and set up an observation post overlooking the ballot post. The afternoon would lead into the evening without a shot fired or a bomb exploding in our vicinity. We would leave our post and return to India Company's forward operating base later that day.

## Deployment III: Operation Iraqi Freedom III

Late one afternoon the following week, we were riding with several Marines from India Company in the back of one of their Humvees. The Humvee was crossing over an open dirt lot in a Fallujah neighborhood when an Iraqi kid began chasing our vehicle. The kid was probably around nine years old as he chased our Humvee hoping to get a handout. The kid was not causing anyone trouble and was smiling as he asked while reaching out.

As the Iraqi kid ran after our Humvee, one of the Marines sitting in the back angrily stood up and shouted, "Get the fuck out of here!" as he pointed his M-16 rifle at the child. The kid's smile immediately transitioned from excitement to terror in a split second as he stopped chasing us. I sat there in disbelief. The Marine who pointed his rifle at the kid appeared to be stressed out and the kid chasing the car was the trigger for the release of his frustration. Would it be a surprise if that child went back home and told his family that an American pointed a gun at him? Would it then be a surprise if someone from that child's family joined the insurgency? I would think not, and that simple act of anger could get Americans killed.

In May of 2005, a contingent of our battalion, along with a team from an Army brigade, discovered a huge weapons cache hidden in the city of Amiriyah, in western Iraq. The cache contained "...more than 4,100 mortar rounds, more than 800 rocket-propelled grenade rounds, more than 100,000 rounds of machine-gun ammunition, 400 grenades, and several thousand pounds of different types of explosives and bomb-making materials" (*https:://www.stripes.com/news/weapons-cache-found-destroyed-in-iraq-1.33009*).

The majority of my third deployment was spent conducting observation post after observation post, as mentioned. However, what made the missions different this time were that the posts were consistently conducted in an urban environment as opposed to the open desert. It seemed almost futile as I am sure the insurgent scouts throughout Fallujah constantly reported on our patrols and observation posts which would prevent enemy fighters from placing IEDs in our fields of view.

There were days of sheer boredom and other days that were more active. There was one incident where one of the coalition checkpoints in Fallujah had been fired at with an AK rifle one afternoon. No one

## 13. Blue on Blue

**Iraqi children greeting me while on foot patrol on the outskirts of Fallujah (May 2005).**

was hurt and the shooter had fled before anyone could fire back apparently. There was also word that one of the Iraqi police stations had been attacked earlier that week and an Iraqi military patrol was hit with an IED. One of the intelligence Marines had access to a photo that depicted the aftermath of the IED attack on the Iraqi vehicle. The photo showed a truck with an Iraqi soldier dead in the bed of the vehicle. The IED shrapnel had torn off the top portion of his head from the mouth up, leaving behind the lower portion of his jaw.

It was apparent that the majority of attacks conducted by the insurgency was against the allied Iraqi military. It was obvious that the insurgents could not win in a stand-up fight against the American military; therefore, the enemy focused on the "softer" targets. Again, this was a similar tactic to those used by the North Vietnamese and Viet Cong during the Vietnam War. I find the similarities between the war in Iraq and Vietnam fascinating, because they show how history can repeat itself.

## Deployment III: Operation Iraqi Freedom III

Throughout the deployment, several of the Iraqi police stations would come under attack from the insurgency as mentioned. It appeared that there was a major effort to undermine the American presence and to destroy the allied Iraqi morale. It was known that many of the "allied" Iraqi forces were playing both sides and we were to trust them "...as far as you could throw them." The war in Iraq was complex while ever evolving with the current political situation. From my understanding, corruption was rife at the highest level.

It was reported that billions of dollars in funds that were supposed to be used to rebuild Iraqi infrastructure had gone missing (*https:// www.theguardian.com/world/2010/jul/27/iraq-oil-funds-billions-missing*). The money was to be used on reconstruction during the 2004–2007 time period; however, the money somehow went unaccounted for. The Iraqi officials claimed that they did not know where that money went. What a huge disservice this was to the people of Iraq whom we were there to help.

I can't say who is ultimately responsible for the misappropriation of the funds, but I can assume that the only people who truly suffered from the lack of accountability were the Iraqi citizens who sought a better life after the invasion. It was obvious that many allowed coalition forces into their neighborhoods and passively supported the allied military effort in a war they thought would bring some prosperity to their country. In my opinion, the early post-invasion years were critical in rebuilding the country and garnering Iraqi support. It seemed unfair to go into a country we were there to help but then not rebuild it with the funds allocated for that purpose.

I believe it was late May 2005 and about 11:00 in the evening when we were suddenly woken up by Marines on watch in Lima Company's forward operating base. Word came down that the CAAT team had been hit by an IED in Lima Company's Area of Operations and that one of their Marines suffered from a severe head injury. Most of Lima Company and our team were dispatched to the town where the IED attack occurred. The Marines loaded up into their Humvees and set out to find out who conducted the incident. Once we reached the neighborhood adjacent to the IED explosion, we disembarked from our vehicles. Lima Company's Commanding Officer exited his

## 13. Blue on Blue

Humvee and appeared very upset. "Get everyone out of their houses! Get every last one of them out!" the Company Commander ordered.

Iraqi civilians were then plucked out of their homes systematically until every house in the surrounding neighborhood had been vacated. Men and male teenagers were separated from the group and detained for questioning. The detainees were separated and sat down in front of their friends and family. Not that we as Marines cared, but it must have been humiliating for the Iraqi men and teenagers to be grabbed out of their homes in the middle of the night and made to sit down like children in a day care.

I understood what Lima Company's Commander was trying to do, but I felt like all we were doing was pissing off the locals and losing their support, if they had any for us at all. The detention and interrogation of the Iraqi males would last throughout the night. I'm not sure if any pertinent information about the IED attack was ever discovered; however, members of the neighborhood knew that we would not take any attack lightly.

Once the interrogations were done, Lima Company and our team would return to the forward operating base. In the following days, my team would set out yet again for another observation post in the area where the recent IED attack against the CAAT team occurred. Our departure was conducted under the cover of darkness as usual and this time we would be accompanied by an Iraqi soldier. After reaching our destination, we had the Iraqi soldier convince an Iraqi family to let us set up our position on their rooftop.

The Iraqi family gave us their permission as we set out onto their home. While occupying our post, the children from the household wanted to hang out with us. We did not have a problem with it. I thought it was a good way to help rebuild some of trust with the Marines and would hopefully keep the family from telling other insurgents about our position.

Sometime early in the morning we heard a loud explosion go off to the rear of our post, maybe fifty yards away. We had not heard the sound of an incoming mortar or rocket round, so we figured an IED that had been placed at an earlier time might have accidentally gone off. There were no American military vehicles in the immediate area.

## Deployment III: Operation Iraqi Freedom III

We got into a defensive posture and scanned the area with our optics; however, nothing out of the ordinary was seen. During our post, the Iraqi family brought us food and coffee as the morning shifted into the afternoon.

As the day ran on, the Iraqi soldier began to get on Travis's nerves. The soldier was somewhat obnoxious, and his tactics were poor. He would walk on our rooftop position in clear view and could have been easily shot if an enemy sniper chose to do so. As tensions built between Travis and the Iraqi soldier, the situation was made worse when one of the older Iraqi children who lived in the home told us that their parents wanted us to leave. Out of respect for the family who supported us for that mission, we left their house and returned to our forward operating base.

The days would go on with intermittent missions conducted in the surrounding palm grove areas without contact or pertinent information to pass on. Much of our free time would be spent working out on the balcony of the forward outpost, reading, and watching DVDs. I think the day in and day out repetition would show on my face. One day while eating lunch outside of the makeshift barracks building, a nearby Marine looked at me and asked if I was ok. I simply told him yes and went back to eating my food. I assume the tension of being on my third Iraq deployment showed and I must admit I felt it to some degree.

# 14.

# Father's Day Massacre

It was mid–2005, when the new Chief Scout for the 3rd Battalion 4th Marines Scout/Sniper platoon asked me, "Brian, are you ok with taking my spot on the OP? I have a meeting with higher." I replied, "Not a problem, Staff Sergeant." He then added, "It'll be a quick one-day mission. You guys will provide over watch for a convoy. The CAAT team will be providing security for some higher ups that will be coming through on the MSR. Once the convoy is through, you guys will be picked up." So, I got my gear ready and packed rather lightly due to the nature of the operation.

Our four-man team had marched out from Lima Company's forward operating base at about midnight, passing through our camp checkpoint and out into the palm groves as usual. We walked through the area until we arrived at our familiar overwatch site at a half-built home. Once there, we all observed the area from our position until we felt comfortable enough that we were not being followed. Marcus took the first security shift and the rest of our four-man team went to sleep.

After sleeping for about four hours, I was woken up by Hank. He was a Scout/Sniper section leader, and it was my turn for security. I stood up half asleep and put on my tactical vest and then grabbed my M-16. I then sat down on a small folding chair and faced the main room that led to the front door. I had my rifle posted within arm's reach against the brick wall and sat down facing the front entrance with my M-9 pistol in my right hand. About an hour and a half into my post, I heard what sounded like the rumbling of thunder. It started rather low and then just gathered momentum into a hellish storm

## Deployment III: Operation Iraqi Freedom III

almost instantly. At that moment I heard the tactical radio come alive. "God damn it, we're being ambushed! We need help god damn it! They're fucking shooting at us!" I never heard a grown man yell like this in my life. It was high pitched, containing fear and desperation at its purest.

This was the sound of a man who knew he was about to die. After hearing the loud thunderous noise that we immediately recognized as gunfire, we knew that at that moment the CAAT team had just been ambushed by insurgents. Without saying it, we all threw on our flak jackets and helmets as fast as we could possibly move. We all felt the urgency and utmost need to gear up to get ready because we knew we were more than likely about to be attacked. After putting on my gear and grabbing my rifle, I ran up the stairs and peered over the half-built wall within the home we occupied. As soon as my head passed the edge of the wall and was visible to the neighboring houses, I heard the crack of a bullet pass by my head. A sniper had just shot at me and then

**Myself watching the "rear" during an observation post in the city of Fallujah (May 2005).**

## 14. Father's Day Massacre

My team sleeping in an observation post in Fallujah (May 2005).

A photograph of me on watch during an observation post in Fallujah (May 2005).

## Deployment III: Operation Iraqi Freedom III

it was confirmed that we had been previously watched, they were simply waiting for us. I said, "Fuck, they know we're here, get ready."

With the gunfire of the large ambush set against the CAAT team about a half mile down the road, we set up in fighting positions within the house. I set up on the top of the stairs watching the room that led to the front entrance. I pulled out the two grenades from my vest as fast as humanly possible. I stripped the safety tape from the grenades and laid the frags next to me should I need them if the enemy fighters attempted to force their way into our position. Marcus and Tom (another member of our section) posted downstairs while watching the rear area that led into the unfenced backyard adjoining the neighboring houses. Hank watched the front yard of the home.

I was crouched into the kneeling position without padding against the hard concrete floor. I wanted to be able to move if necessary, had the insurgents gained entry into the house. As we waited, I looked downstairs for clues as to what the other guys were seeing. Marcus got my attention with an almost inaudible "Hey." "We have four guys, in one car. All armed and with RPG's hanging out of the windows, just passed the house on the main road."

Apparently, the enemy fighters were getting into positions near our house. Hank then turned around and gave us the hand signal showing two fingers, indicating that there were two other insurgents near the front yard. He then acted like he was holding something large on his back depicting that the enemy fighters had RPGs and machine guns on their backs. We then knew, without any doubt in our minds, that we were in for the fight of our lives. It was about to get up close and brutal.

We remained in our positions while listening to the battle taking place down the road. I continued to sit on my right knee and looked down my rifle sights, waiting for someone to enter the front room. The level of panic and fear was rising. It was felt by all four of us. My mouth was extremely dry as I waited for bullets along with rocket propelled grenades to rip through the walls of the house we occupied. It was surprisingly quiet in our immediate area, especially having seen the insurgents walk directly in front of our building and the sniper shot earlier.

## 14. Father's Day Massacre

My position overlooking the front door of our post during the "Father's Day Massacre" battle (June 2005).

# Deployment III: Operation Iraqi Freedom III

The fear I felt was suddenly interrupted when I heard Marcus subtly say, "Hey Gordo!" I looked over as he took a sip from a plastic water bottle. He then tossed the bottle my way. His mouth must have been dry too and he must have known that I needed some water as well. I quickly drank from the bottle and tossed it back to him.

I then immediately regained focus onto my rifle sights and continued to wait for enemy fighters to rush in. I had a feeling that an assault was coming, and I remained focused on the main entry. My whole train of thought was that we were likely dead men. The insurgents MUST have known we were in that building and were figuring out a plan to try and kill us. A part of me deep down inside just wanted to run out of our position. Maybe it was the sheer fear of dying that was creating that thought.

However, I knew if that happened, I would simply be shot down by the insurgents waiting nearby. I also couldn't leave my buddies. If I was going to die, I was galvanized by the idea to remain where I was and take out as many of them as I could before they could try to kill me. The adrenaline continued to rise as the fighting down the road with the CAAT team raged on. I had maybe one month left before I was to return home.

How would my family feel if I were killed in combat? What would I miss out on in my life? Would the insurgents simply place an AK-47 around the door and spray into our building? Or would they simply shred the place with rocket propelled grenades? I couldn't help but sit there and think that a rocket would rip into the wall where I sat. The thought of seeing my good friends maimed or killed right in front of me raced through my mind as well. I then felt anger building up in my body over the idea of being killed with my friends only one month before going home.

An insurgent then walked into our building and in front of my sights as he entered the front door. I was in disbelief at how nonchalantly he entered the room in front of me while holding his AK-47 in his right hand. He wore a red face wrap and black clothing with sandals. At the moment he made entry, I shot him square in the chest with my M-16. I saw his life immediately leave his body as he collapsed to the brick floor. Knowing that there was likely a whole enemy team just

## 14. Father's Day Massacre

on the other side of the wall in the adjacent room, I quickly grabbed a nearby grenade, pulled the pin, and tossed it over the wall into the other room.

There was a brief three-second pause followed by an explosion. It was extremely loud and dust from the concussive blast rushed into our room, through the gaps in the brick wall. Marcus then immediately tossed another grenade into the same area. It looked as though he tossed the grenade like a hook shot in basketball. Again, there was a pause followed by a large explosion with a gust of dirt rushing into our room.

This shock wave from Marcus' grenade forced another fighter into my sights near the main entry as he tried to flee the bombarded section of the home. He was holding a medium machine gun, an RPK. I immediately shot him twice in the chest. Once he collapsed, I shot him in the back as he lay on the floor. He had fallen near the AK-47 and RPK. I did not want him grabbing either and using those weapons to shoot me. After killing the second combatant, I tossed another grenade into the adjacent room to flush out whoever remained.

Shortly after the explosion, I could hear shooting just below me where Tom and Marcus had set up. "They're fucking running across the field!" I heard Marcus say. Both Tom and Marcus were shooting at the insurgent fighters after they fled from our building and ran out into the rear open yard. I then heard a loud explosion. Marcus had launched a grenade from his M203 launcher which then hit a nearby tree. I shouted downstairs, "Fuck them up! Keep it up!"

We were fighting like wild men. People were dying and we did not want to be next. We felt like tigers with our backs against the wall and we had to fight like mad to make it out alive. I prayed very hard silently in my head as Tom got on the radio and said in a nervous tone, "We are engaged in continuous combat! We need QRF now!" I prayed so hard that it almost physically hurt.

Marcus and Tom continued shooting towards the rear open yard behind our building, conducting speed reloads. "Cover me, changing mags out!" Then the other would pick up the pace of fire. After a few minutes of Tom and Marcus shooting, Marcus said, "Shit, we are low on ammo!" Suddenly it felt like the whole city opened up on

## Deployment III: Operation Iraqi Freedom III

us. The deafening roar of multiple machine guns and AK-47s ripped off angrily at our position. It sounded as if the entire neighborhood was shooting at us. I thought, "This is it. I am dead." I simply waited for bullets and rockets to pierce the walls to finish us off; however, I remained in my position, fixated on the front room. Several mortar rounds landed near our building followed by their concussive blasts. It was mass chaos.

Tom continued to request QRF support for our beleaguered position. Eventually I heard the roaring of vehicle engines just outside of our post from inside the house. It was the CAAT team that had been ambushed earlier. Machine guns from Humvees and enemy combatants ripped off just outside of our position. I then heard the sound of an RPG being fired off followed by a loud metallic ping. The firing from both sides continued for about another five minutes and eventually waned off.

Shortly after, Marines from the Humvee team dismounted and hurried into our building to check on us. I was never so relieved to see other Marines in my life. As they walked in, they immediately saw the dead fighters on the floor. One of the Marines stated, "Holy shit, you guys did this?!" We told them how the insurgents attempted to fight their way into our post and how we fought them off. We also told them that we needed ammo. Their lieutenant, whom I heard on the radio earlier at the start of the battle, immediately threw down several magazines onto the floor and told his Marines to immediately mount up to continue the fight. Word came down that the QRF team from Lima Company's base had been ambushed as well when they responded to the battle. The CAAT lieutenant told us to hold our positions and that they would return for us.

As we held our positions, I heard a helicopter approaching our area from a distance. When it eventually came into view overhead, I immediately recognized it as a Marine gunship. I believe it was a Super Stallion equipped with a .50 caliber machine gun at the opened rear hatch. Once I saw the gunship, I immediately pulled out my flashing beacon hoping that the pilot and gunner could see that we occupied a friendly position. Every part of me prayed that the gunner would not fire on us, mistaking us for enemy combatants. The helicopter continued to circle

## 14. Father's Day Massacre

above and thankfully did not fire at our position. There was a feeling that the battle was almost over, which was confirmed when no other shots were fired. There was a great sense of relief.

It was almost a spiritual moment when I knew it was likely that I was going to survive the battle and that the worst of it was over. I felt a lineage to the hardship that other Marines have endured in past battles, as I only obtained a glimpse of it. The Marine Corps hymn was going through my mind and my heart felt the words of what I believe the song meant to portray. It was an almost indescribable euphoric feeling; maybe it was from all the adrenaline or the relief of having survived close combat.

As we waited, Tom and Hank cleared the front of the house. There they found a partially set up Russian NSV heavy machine gun alongside a metal mounting system. The heavy machine gun was likely being put in place by the insurgents to continue the ambush on the CAAT team. However, they were not able to finish the job due to my

**AK-74 medium and butterfly grip Russian model heavy machine gun recovered from dead enemy fighters during the "Father's Day Massacre" (June 2005).**

## Deployment III: Operation Iraqi Freedom III

team's occupation of the building and the fight that took place there. Or it was possible that the heavy machine gun was about to be used on my team's position and was disrupted by the CAAT team as they came to our sieged position during the battle. Either way, that type of weaponry would have caused some serious damage had it been utilized that day.

Once the CAAT team returned and pulled up alongside our building, our team made its way out of the house. We couldn't thank them enough for what they had done coming to our aid. We told them we had heard the fighting outside of the house when they arrived and asked what the loud metallic ping was. One of the CAAT Marines pointed at a nearby Humvee turret manned by one of their men. There was a dent on the turret where an RPG rocket had ricocheted against the metal. Apparently, the rocket had hit the circular turret at enough of an angle to not detonate and kill the Marine.

While we spoke to the CAAT Marines, I noticed that they had stacked the dead insurgent bodies from the initial ambush onto the front of some of their Humvees. The two enemy combatants that I had killed were removed from our building and stacked onto the hood of a nearby vehicle. As one of the Marines was placing one of the bodies onto his Humvee, he removed the fighter's watch from his wrist. "Here's a souvenir," the Marine said as he handed me the deceased combatant's watch. I never believed in taking personal war souvenirs from dead enemy combatants, but I took the watch anyway.

After deeming the area secure, the CAAT task force along with our team got into the Humvees and proceeded to drive through the nearby town. There were about five Humvees, and each had recently killed insurgents stacked onto their hoods, about thirty bodies total. It must have been a brutal scene as our vehicles drove through the Iraqi neighborhood. Many Iraqi citizens had been standing on the side of the road and were looking at us as we passed through town. The plan was to take the dead enemy combatants back to friendly lines where they could be searched for intelligence; however, the display of the bodies also served as a warning to other insurgents who might be watching.

After arriving at Lima Company's forward operating base, we

## 14. Father's Day Massacre

exited the CAAT platoon's Humvee. I turned to the driver and while shaking his hand thanked him for basically saving my life. I had never felt such a sense of gratitude toward a group of people in my life and to this day I'm not sure my Scout/Sniper team would have made it out of that battle alive had it not been for the bravery of those men.

I felt exhausted, likely from the huge adrenaline spike during the fight. Our team made our way into the base and found a large couch to sit on. We just sat there and kind of laughed at what we had just been through. I was grateful to be alive and I could see the exhaustion as well on Tom's face. He just sat there and smoked a cigarette while looking down at the floor.

The reality of the battle set in. The incident was different because the fighting had initially been so close for me. I had previously taken the lives of other combatants through the lens of a scope. It was a personal experience then; however, it was even more so when the enemy you shot was only feet away, as opposed to yards.

I eventually found out that the CAAT team had been ambushed by four machine gun nests when the Father's Day ambush started. The insurgents attempted to push the CAAT team onto an IED laden road; however, the Marines charged at their fortified positions instead. Some members of the team even dismounted from their vehicles and began throwing grenades into the enemy bunkers. The CAAT team was estimated to have killed about thirty insurgents and sent many to nearby hospitals where they were later detained (*http://marinecorpsmars.net/Honors%20Pages/References/wyatt_waldron.htm*).

Marcus had also told me that he observed several dead insurgents within several yards of our defensive position at the end of the battle when he conducted a walk through with CAAT Marines. It was a combination of kills from Marcus, Tom, me, and the CAAT team when they arrived at our position. Upon hearing all the details of the battle, it was still amazing that no Americans involved in that firefight were killed. It was also revealed that the CAAT team which came to our aid during the battle consciously drove past a vehicle IED that was positioned on the side of the road. They knew the vehicle was likely an IED and they drove past it anyway to get to our position that was under heavy attack. When the CAAT team drove past the Iraqi car, it

## Deployment III: Operation Iraqi Freedom III

detonated and flames entered the passenger compartment of one of their Humvees, yet they still pushed on to help us.

The dead insurgent bodies from the battle earlier that morning had been placed in black body bags near Lima Company's headquarters detachment building. The bodies were laid out in a linear pattern, side by side. While looking at the bodies, I found the chest rig from one of the fighters I shot. One of my M-16 rifle rounds punctured his full AK magazine and blew it out into his chest.

I called my family later that afternoon. I initially spoke with my mother and for some reason I felt that it was necessary to tell her what happened that morning. A part of me felt that it was important for them to know what was going on here. I gave a quick synopsis of the firefight that took place, and I heard her begin to cry. She tried to piece together words as she told me that she loved me and did not want anything to happen to me. My stepfather then got on the phone and spoke with me. His voice cracked as he tried to tell me to be safe. It hurt to hear them so sad, but I kept reassuring them that I was ok and would continue to be safe.

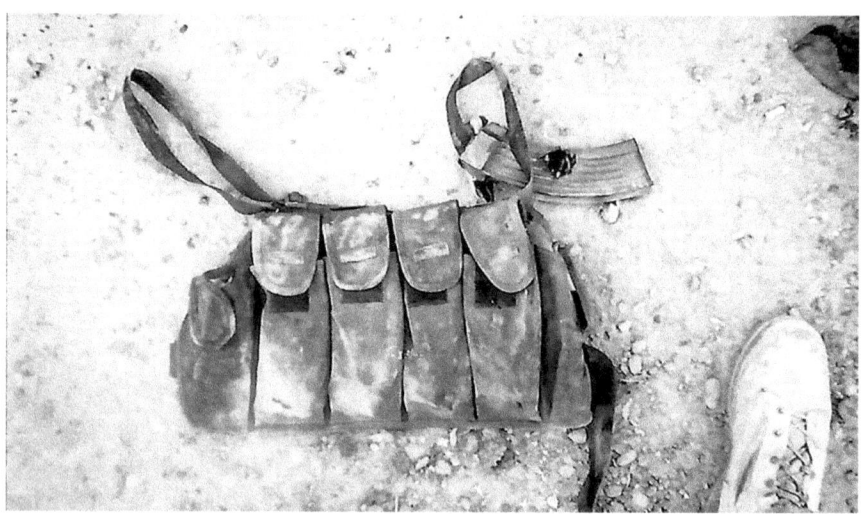

**AK magazine chest rig worn by an enemy combatant during the "Father's Day Massacre." The 5.56mm round impact that I fired can be seen in the AK magazine (June 2005).**

## 14. Father's Day Massacre

I spoke to a Marine from Lima Company that day who had been ambushed during the battle. He mentioned that he was part of the QRF that was coming to help during the fight. He then mentioned how they were fired upon from the side of the road shortly after leaving base camp. Their squad was ambushed as they drove in their QRF Humvee. The squad then returned fire, killing at least two enemy combatants. I was surprised at the level of coordination by the insurgent fighters and how they anticipated the American reaction.

They knew to set up on the CAAT team, then somehow knew to surround the Scout/Sniper position, and then reacted to the QRF response. The insurgents obviously expected the QRF team to come to the battle. Even though the enemy coordination seemed well planned, they failed to kill any of the Marines during the fight. Every portion of the ambush was repelled by the Americans and turned against them. The Marines in that battle killed approximately thirty insurgents. The enemy combatants were well armed with assault rifles, medium to heavy machine guns, rockets, and mortars.

I was thankful to be alive and thankful that there were well trained Marines who fought in that battle. We were also very lucky. The enemy had the initiative, and the battle could have easily been in their favor; however, the situation somehow worked to our advantage and against the enemy combatant's will. Looking back, the battle was brutal and desperate. All the Marines involved fought hard for their lives and came out on top.

Some of the Marines involved in the fight were awarded medals and were recognized for their valor. The CAAT team involved fought off an ambush by a large enemy force who shot at them from fortified positions. After repelling that enemy attack, they drove through a vehicle IED to get to my position and fought off the enemy who ambushed us there as well as resupplying my team. They then responded to the QRF team who had been attacked.

# 15

# Home and Comfort

News had come in that several female Marines had been killed by a vehicle borne IED. The female Marines, I believe, were part of a K-9 search team that was attached to Kilo Company at a checkpoint located in the west neighborhoods of Fallujah. Rumor was that the female Marines had been wearing their headphones during a convoy when they were hit by the IED. When the Marines found their bodies, the headphones had been burnt into their heads by the blast of the car bomb.

Having heard about the headphones being worn while on a convoy in the middle of Fallujah, I thought of the complacency that may have existed during that incident. I was thinking how can any Marine put headphones on in the middle of a city that had been home to the largest battle since the start of the Iraq War? Yes, it was quiet at times, and attacks were not daily. However, it was known that insurgents were still taking potshots at Marines and consistently setting up IEDs along the roads for use against the American military.

I think that it is fair to say that the insurgents targeted American convoys that looked "less prepared" or complacent. I'm not saying that the convoy I just mentioned could have done anything different, because it seemed that they were simply in the wrong place at the wrong time. With that being said, the enemy combatants likely ambushed the Marines who did not seem concerned with facing outboard with their weapons trained at the ready should any danger expose itself. Or attacking the convoys that took the same route consistently at around the same time of the day/night. Regardless, it was disheartening to hear while so close to returning to the United States.

## 15. Home and Comfort

A week after the Father's Day battle, our team prepared yet again for another night observation post along an MSR running through the western portion of Fallujah. We loaded up our four-man team onto the back of one of Lima Company's Humvees in the front of the forward operating base. There was an additional Humvee being mounted by a security squad from Lima Company. The security squads' job was to provide protection for our insertion in case of an enemy ambush. It was roughly ten in the evening as we were cleared to leave the main entrance of the base.

As we traveled along the road, the Humvee vehicle lights were off as usual, and we made our way along the nearby river. The vehicles eventually made their way to the designated drop-off point for our post. Our team dismounted the Humvee and we walked to our previously scouted position. Our area was a small abandoned two-story building near the town water pump facility which overlooked the MSR.

Approximately one minute after dismounting our Humvee, we heard a pop. The noise was very loud, and I initially thought we had been shot at. No one knew for sure what it was, and I was somewhat shaken up. My heart was racing, and my adrenaline rose as it had on previous occasions. After the Father's Day Massacre and so close to returning home, I was leery of another ambush. No one in the patrol could really figure out what had just happened, so our team set up in the original observation position as previously planned, while the patrol continued driving away from our insertion area.

After getting into position, we conducted our typical two-hour watch rotations. The evening was uneventful until we reached early daylight. It was about seven in the morning when the radio came alive with transmissions from a CAAT patrol in the area. The CAAT team had stumbled upon the item that had made the loud pop the previous evening. It was an unexploded IED. The IED must have been a dud and the loud pop we heard was the blasting cap being set off by a nearby insurgent. The unexploded IED was a 155mm artillery shell wired for detonation. It was eerie to think that we had come so close to being hit by a large bomb in an open vehicle. Had that munition successfully exploded when the blasting cap was set off, an entire fire team from Lima Company would have been blown to pieces.

## Deployment III: Operation Iraqi Freedom III

The remainder of the deployment would be filled with observation posts and foot patrols up until those last few weeks. It seemed that time almost slowed down the last month because I knew I was so close to returning home. With that being said, my anxiety level would slightly go up because I did not want anything to happen that would jeopardize my safe return to the United States. I think almost all the Marines deployed felt that way when getting so close to going home.

The 3rd Battalion 4th Marines would eventually be replaced by another Marine Corps unit in Fallujah. We would conduct the "left seat, right seat" operations until the replacement battalion was familiar with the area. Our unit would then regroup at Camp Fallujah where it would make its way back to an allied air base where we would fly into Kuwait. It was always an exciting time when the order to move out of a combat area was given. We knew that we would be going home in a short time and the stress of constantly conducting operations would dissipate.

Once the battalion arrived in Kuwait, there was a sense of relaxation and ease. The unit would stay there for about a week where Marines could get rest and eat plenty of hot meals. It might as well have been a vacation. I was very into lifting weights and the idea of eating four hot meals a day (to include the midnight rations) was a welcome prospect. The gyms on camp in Kuwait were all modern and there were plenty of supplements being sold at the exchange.

Treatment in Kuwait was always exceptional. Not much would be asked of us other than to account for each other on a daily basis and to go through customs without incident. We were allowed to roam the base, watch movies, read, and listen to music. The battalion would then make its way back to Kuwait International Airport where we would fly out of the Middle East while making stops in Germany, Maryland, and then California.

Upon landing at March Air Force Base, I could not help but feel overwhelmed with a sense of accomplishment and comfort. I just survived a horrible battle during the last month of my deployment and from what I knew, I was home for good, never to return to Iraq. As we walked off the airplane and down the stairs, I recall seeing the rolling hills of Moreno Valley in the afternoon sun. It was a welcome sight

## 15. Home and Comfort

compared to months of palm groves and blown out buildings. I also felt a sense of ease. I would no longer have to look for roadside bombs or worry about sporadic small-arms ambushes, and I could eat a good home cooked meal.

As I and the other Marines from my unit entered the airport processing area, we were warmly greeted by members of the Veterans of Foreign Wars (VFW) post. They were elderly and looked genuinely happy to see us. I was just as happy to see them as well. As we waited for the buses to arrive to take us back to the Twenty-Nine Palms Marine Corps base, we snacked on the food that the VFW had kindly provided us. Everyone was just happy; you could feel it from everyone there. We knew we were home, and the feeling of excitement was contagious.

The buses would arrive at the air base after only a few hours. Everyone hurriedly got onto the buses with their carry-on bags that they had with them from the airplane ride. As the buses departed, Marines listened to their headphones, others joked, some talked about what they were going to do when they finally got liberty, and others were simply quiet, just looking out of their respective windows from the bus. I was looking out of my window at the nearby neighborhoods and just thinking how good it was to be home.

As the bus ride went on, we arrived in the Joshua Tree area after about two hours. Joshua Tree was maybe a half-hour drive from the Marine Corps Air Ground Combat Center. The driver had a local rock music station playing over the speakers on the bus. It seemed that at the moment we arrived in Joshua Tree, on the long stretch of road leading to Twenty-Nine Palms, Ozzy Osbourne's "Mama I'm Coming Home" song played on the radio. Everyone was quiet as the guitar intro played and filled the bus.

It gave me goosebumps because of the song's timing. Here are a bunch of 19 to 20-year-old young men coming home from overseas and a song about returning home to a mother comes on. "Times have changed, and times are strange, here I come, but I ain't the same, Mama, I'm coming home." It was simply quiet, and we just listened. It seemed as if no one spoke a word and just absorbed what was being played on the speakers. It was true, I was coming home, and I was not

## Deployment III: Operation Iraqi Freedom III

the same. A part of me was gone forever in Iraq. The rampant death, almost dying, losing friends / colleagues, and having killed others changed a part of me forever.

It was ironic, because the song I recall hearing for my first deployment to Iraq was ""Cat's in the Cradle" by Harry Chapin during the flight to Kuwait. Then to hear Ozzy Osbourne's song upon returning home from what was to be my final combat deployment seemed to fit with what I experienced during the war. It was almost spiritual because it felt like my Iraq War experience came full circle. It felt as if a burden had been lifted and in a sense it was true.

The buses the battalion rode in would drive into the Marine Corps Air Ground Combat Center yet again. As with the previous deployments, friends and family would again greet us. When I saw my family, they were there with a large cooler of beer. My buddies and I grabbed a drink, and it was probably the best tasting beer I ever had. Everyone there was just happy, and it is just one of those experiences that I will never forget. I feel truly grateful to have felt that alive.

Soon after returning home, my parents threw a welcome home pool party for my platoon in their backyard. There was plenty of alcohol and the feeling overall was one of relief. Almost everyone at the celebration had imbibed to the point of being drunk. Later in the evening, as the party wore on, Mason started talking to me about Jose and how the events unfolded just before his death. He mentioned how the Recon team assaulted their position with a mounted machine gun and struck Jose with their Humvee. He then mentioned how he had to remove the dirt from Jose's mouth and face while breaking down into tears as he struggled to finish the story.

Other members of the platoon who were listening to Mason speak about Jose became emotional as well. About four of us hugged, shed some tears, and said how much we missed him. It was a bond I have yet to share with anyone I've known since then. These guys were special to me, and I will forever see them as my brothers.

After celebrating our return home, the platoon and I went to visit Jose's family in Simi Valley in the summer of 2005. The weather was sunny and warm when we met with his mother at the cemetery where he was laid to rest. The platoon gathered around his grave site and

## 15. Home and Comfort

stood there quietly. It felt kind of weird being home and happy while knowing that Jose did not make it back to see his family or his fiancée. We were all home, but he was the only one from our battalion that did not return alive from the previous deployment.

As we walked away from Jose's site and toward our cars, I saw his mother sitting down next to his headstone while looking down at the ground toward him. I could tell that she missed him very much and it struck a nerve with me seeing her longing for her son. I tried very hard not to show my emotions, but tears streamed down my face as I tried to quickly wipe them away from under my sunglasses. It was tough to see her looking down at his resting place and to know that thousands of other mothers like her had likely done the same thing when they had lost their sons or daughters during the Iraq War.

After visiting Jose and his family, the Scout/Sniper platoon members would split off in different directions in life. Some members, including me, would soon get out of the Marine Corps, while others stayed with the platoon to conduct another Iraq deployment. Prior to getting out, I had been offered a chance to become part of the Marine Corps Explosive Ordnance Detachment teams. I respectfully refused as I knew that would mean future deployments in which my job would be to hunt for roadside bombs. No thanks, I had enough of war.

In retrospect, the Iraq War was the most brutal conflict Americans had found themselves in since Vietnam. The casualties were thankfully not as high as that engagement; however, there was a large burden placed on a relatively small number of troops over an entire country. American military personnel killed in action ran into the thousands and those injured/maimed went into the tens of thousands. I would think that the casualty figures would have been higher for the United States had it not been for the advancements in combat medicine and technology since the 1960s.

As in my previous returns to the United States, I would take my leave and visit my family. There was that time for reflection on what I experienced overseas and many times I would wake up in the middle of the night in shock of what I experienced. I wouldn't wake up screaming or anything of that nature. The events of the Father's Day

## Deployment III: Operation Iraqi Freedom III

battle would simply replay in my mind, and I would lie there and think, "Shit, that really happened."

One afternoon in the fall of 2005 while visiting my parents, I was in their backyard and sitting with them. We had some small talk as the conversation transitioned to some of my experiences in Iraq. My mom then asked me about Jose and the situation that led to his death. I began telling her and at that moment, I broke down while trying to fight back my emotions. I cried and quickly reined in my tears by wiping my eyes. It was difficult to talk about him and I realized how much I kept inside. My third Iraq deployment had been the toughest so far.

My divorce with Stephanie would eventually be finalized, which had greatly affected me prior to the third deployment. Then I had experienced the loss of a friend who I had trained with day in and day out for over a year. This was followed by a brutal battle that took place on Father's Day in which my friends and I almost lost our lives. It was a tough period in my life; however, I was still excited to be home and live my life, not only for myself, but for those who did not have the chance to do so. Those whose lives were cut short in a long war.

The 3rd Battalion 4th Marines Scout/Sniper platoon would go on to another Operation Iraqi Freedom tour by the time I got out of the Marine Corps. That deployment would be a tough one for the battalion, as I later found out they suffered quite a few casualties near the Syrian border. Dean would go on to lose both of his legs due to an IED attack on the Humvee he was traveling in. It bothered me that I did not go on that deployment with the Scout/Sniper platoon because we had gone through so much together.

I would later visit the platoon when they returned from their most recent Iraq deployment in early 2007. When they finally got off the buses at the Twenty-Nine Palms base, we all just gave each other big hugs. I could tell they had been through a lot. Later that evening, Hank, Dalton, Travis, and I went out to the local bar near base. We were all sitting at a small table speaking amongst ourselves until we were suddenly interrupted by, "Hey, you guys are fucking POGs!" We looked around to see who was talking and found two Marines looking in our direction from a nearby table.

"You guys are fucking POGs, aren't you?!" the young Marine

## 15. Home and Comfort

stated again. Our group looked at each other as if the guy was crazy. Our guys were all school trained Scout/Snipers, with the exception of myself, who all had three combat deployments each to Iraq. Hank then replies, "What the fuck?! Are you serious?!" while we all laughed at the apparent arrogance of the young Marine making his assumption. The young Marine in his unrelenting drunken state then said, "Fuck you, you guys are fucking POGs" as he then challenged Hank to a fight.

In short, our group walked outside of the bar as the young Marine brought his friends to meet with us. A melee broke out in the parking lot and Marines were punching, kneeing, and wrestling each other. I specifically recall Dalton grabbing one of the Marines behind the neck and kneeing him directly in the face. During the fight, one of the bar employees yelled out from the rear door of the business and said she called the sheriffs. We all then got into our car and drove away from the bar. That was the most recent time I've seen so many members of the Scout/Sniper platoon together. Since then, we have kept in touch via text messages through our cell phones throughout the years.

Some of the men who served with me in the Scout/Sniper platoon during the Iraq War would go on to become part of MARSOC (Marine Corps Special Operations Command), work as special operators with the United States Army, serve as a military helicopter pilot, become an employee within the space/aeronautics industry, serve as firefighters/police officers, and become authors. It was an honor to have served with every one of them.

It was weird to think that from all the recent chaos I experienced during the war, I was alive to see my home again. I was alive to start a new chapter in my life and build. I just hope that the sacrifice made by the American military, my friends, and my family was worth it. I also hope that the sacrifices made by the Iraqis who were on our side were worth it. Our Iraqi allies were the ones who suffered the most and it was their homeland that had been torn apart by the war. I had met some good people over there and those who only wanted what was best for their families. I hope they get the peace and prosperity that they sacrificed so much for during that war.

# Military History of the Author

My date of enlistment was February of 2002 at Marine Corps Recruit Depot (MCRD) San Diego, CA. Upon completion of Marine Corps bootcamp, I attended the Camp Pendleton School of Infantry at around June of 2002 for approximately two months. I was assigned to the 3rd battalion 4th marines (7th Marine Regiment, 1st Marine Division) at 29 Palms Marine Corps Air Ground Combat Center (MCAGCC) around September of 2002. I was initially assigned as infantry platoon radio operator with Kilo Company and first deployed to Kuwait for preparation of Operation Iraqi Freedom in January of 2003. My unit invaded Iraq for Operation Iraqi Freedom in March of 2003 as part of the 1st Marine Expeditionary Force (1 MEF). After Iraqi Freedom, I deployed with 3rd battalion 4th Marines to Okinawa with the Scout / Sniper platoon (Headquarters Company) as a team leader and PIG (Professionally Instructed Gunman) in September 2003. In March of 2004, I redeployed back to Iraq (Operation Iraqi Freedom 2) and participated in Operation Vigilant Resolve (First Battle of Fallujah) which took place in April of 2004. After returning to 29 Palms, I was again ordered to return to Fallujah, Iraq (Operation Iraqi Freedom 3) with the 3rd battalion 4th Marines for a third combat tour under the operational command of the 2nd Marine Division. I was honorably discharged from the Marines in February 2006.

I was recalled for active service with the Marine Corps in 2008 upon completing my probation period with LAPD. I was assigned to the 1st Marine Expeditionary Force Headquarters Group and was sent to Fallujah, Iraq, for my 4th combat tour.

## Military History of the Author

My ranks included private (E1) upon completion of bootcamp, private first class (E2) when I was initially assigned to 3rd Battalion 4th Marines, lance corporal (E3) during my first deployment to Kuwait for Operation Iraqi Freedom, corporal (E4) during my last year of enlistment, and then sergeant (E5) when I was recalled in 2008.

# Acronyms and Other Abbreviations

**AAV**   Assault Amphibious Vehicle

**AT**   Anti-Tan

**BDU**   Battle Dress Uniform

**CAAT**   Combined Anti-Armor Team

**DI**   Drill Instructor

**EOD**   Explosive Ordnance Disposal

**FAC**   Forward Air Controller

**FOB**   Forward Operating Base

**GPS**   Global Positioning System

**HOG**   Hunter of Gunmen

**HVT**   High Value Target

**IED**   Improvised Explosive Device

**MCAGCC**   Marine Corps Air Ground Combat Center

**MCMAP**   Marine Corps Martial Arts Program

**MCRD**   Marine Corps Recruit Depot

**MOPP**   Mission Oriented Protective Posture

**MOS**   Military Occupational Specialty

**MOUT**   Military Operation on Urban Terrain

**MCT**   Marine Combat Training

**MCX**   Marine Corps Exchange

## Acronyms and Other Abbreviations

**MLRS**  Multiple Launch Rocket System

**MRE**  Meal Ready to Eat

**MSR**  Main Supply Route

**NCO**  Non-Commissioned Officer

**ODA**  Operational Detachment Alpha

**OP**  Observation Post

**PIG**  Professionally Instructed Gunman

**POG**  Person Other than Grunt

**PT**  Physical Training

**QRF**  Quick Reaction Force

**RPG**  Rocket Propelled Grenade

**SASR**  Special Application Scoped Rifle

**SAW**  Squad Automatic Weapon

**SOI**  School of Infantry

**SOTG**  Special Operations Training Group

**VBIED**  Vehicle Borne Improvised Explosive Device

**VFW**  Veterans of Foreign Wars

**U.S.**  United States

# Index

Abrams  39, 49, 99
Abu Ghraib (Iraq)  140, 141
AC-130  106, 114
AK-47  89, 154, 155
Al-Asad (Iraq)  86
ambush  47, 54, 58, 80, 82, 86, 87, 103, 109, 113, 115, 117, 118, 120, 127, 130–132, 137, 143, 150, 152, 156–159, 161–163, 165
Amphibious  39–41, 173
artillery  37, 39, 45, 47, 52, 53, 65, 74, 82, 88, 90, 100, 101, 117, 118, 163
Azerbaijan  83

Baghdad (Iraq)  40, 43, 45–48, 54, 56–63, 65
Blackwater  86
boot camp  3–16, 18, 19
Bridgeport (CA)  69, 71, 72

Camp Fallujah (Iraq)  87, 88, 90, 112, 113, 127, 128, 134–136, 164
Camp Pendleton (CA)  3, 10, 15, 16, 18–20, 28, 66, 79, 171
Camp Schwab (Okinawa, Japan)  79, 80, 82
Camp Victory (Kuwait)  82, 83
combatant  42, 49, 58, 62, 85, 94, 97, 99, 101, 128, 129, 143, 155, 156, 158–162
Combined Anti-Armor Team (CAAT)  84, 120, 146, 147, 149, 150, 152, 154, 156–159, 161, 163, 173
corpsman  6, 26, 48, 53, 61
CS gas  97, 99

Diyala (Iraq)  47–51, 53, 55, 58
Dunham, Jason  75, 113, 114

engineers  53, 54
Explosive Ordnance Disposal (EOD)  132, 173

1st Battalion 3rd Marines (1/3)  128–130
Forward Air Controller (FAC)  95–97, 173
Forward Operating Base (FOB)  84, 87, 90, 129, 131, 132, 143, 146–149, 158, 163, 173

H & S Company (Headquarters & Service)  23, 100
High Value Target (HVT)  84, 173,
Hunter of Gunmen (HOG)  66, 68–70, 72, 173

Improvised Explosive Device (IED)  45, 55, 56, 82–85, 87, 112, 113, 115–119, 130, 134–137, 143–147, 159, 161–163, 168, 173
India Company  128, 130–132, 138, 143, 144
infrared  106

Karma (Iraq)  113
Kilo Company  23–25, 27, 31, 36, 38, 39, 42–45, 47–49, 51–53, 56–59, 62, 66, 67, 71, 75, 85, 87–90, 93, 97, 101–103, 113, 120, 132, 162, 171
Kuwait International Airport  63, 164

Lima Company  110–112, 114, 146, 147, 149, 156, 158, 160, 161, 163

M-16  5, 6, 18, 28, 66, 105, 110, 115, 118, 137, 140, 144, 149, 154, 160
M-40  69, 79, 89, 91, 97, 104, 140

# Index

Main Supply Route (MSR)  45, 90, 91, 93, 102, 104, 107, 108, 115–119, 127–129, 134, 136, 137, 149, 163, 174
Marine Corps Air Ground Combat Center (MCAGCC) (CA)  21, 23, 27, 64, 73, 74, 165, 166, 171, 173
Marine Corps Martial Arts Program (MCMAP)  7, 173
Marine Corps Recruit Depot (MCRD) (CA)  3–5, 8–10, 13, 14, 171, 173
Marine Expeditionary Force (MEF)  47, 48, 171
Marlantes, Karl  1
Military Operations on Urban Terrain (MOUT)  20, 25, 28, 29, 90, 173
Mojave Desert (CA)  22
mortars  26, 27, 43, 45, 48–50, 110, 161
Mujahedeen  101, 117

Navy  5, 6

Operation Iraqi Freedom  168, 171, 172
Operation Vigilant Resolve  87, 96, 171
Operational Detachment Alpha (ODA)  119, 120, 174
overwatch  95, 102, 104, 107, 130, 134, 136, 143, 149

Pentagon  1, 19
Professionally Instructed Gunman (PIG)  71, 72, 114, 171, 174

Quick Reaction Force (QRF)  117, 118, 155, 156, 161, 174

reconnaissance  58, 84, 85, 115–117
recruits  3–5, 7–13
Regimental Combat Team  1, 87

satchel charge  98, 99
School of Infantry (SOI)  13–21, 24, 28, 171, 174
7th Marines  72, 75, 109, 110, 114
Special Application Scoped Rifle (SASR)  103, 115, 174
Special Operations Training Group (SOTG)  79, 80, 174

3rd Battalion 4th Marines (3/4)  20, 22, 23, 38, 47, 66, 68, 69, 73, 75, 82, 83, 86, 110, 114, 122, 128, 130, 149, 164, 168, 171, 172

Vehicle Borne Improvised Explosive Device (VBIED)  45, 55, 56, 112, 134, 162, 174
Veterans of Foreign Wars (VFW)  165, 174

*Wall Street Journal*  54

Zodiac  85

www.ingramcontent.com/pod-product-compliance
Ingram Content Group UK Ltd.
Pitfield, Milton Keynes, MK11 3LW, UK
UKHW042015140426
5217IPUK00015B/1184